**TALES OF TERROR'S
DECADES OF TERROR 2020
2000S HORROR MOVIES**

Copyright © 2020 by Steve Hutchison
All rights reserved. This book or any portion thereof may not be reproduced or used in any manner whatsoever without the express written permission of the publisher except for the use of brief quotations in a book review or scholarly journal.

First Printing: 2020
ISBN-13: 978-1704587011

Bookstores and wholesalers: Please contact books@terror.ca.

Tales of Terror
tales@terror.ca
www.terror.ca

CONTENTS

12	HANNIBAL
13	SAW
14	1408
15	THE OTHERS
16	THE BUTTERFLY EFFECT
17	HOUSE OF WAX
18	DRAG ME TO HELL
19	CLUB DREAD
20	DEATH PROOF
21	HOLLOW MAN
22	FINAL DESTINATION
23	FINAL DESTINATION 3
24	SAW II
25	FINAL DESTINATION 2
26	DAWN OF THE DEAD
27	GINGER SNAPS
28	SCREAM 3
29	AMERICAN PSYCHO
30	THE HOLE
31	WILLARD
32	FRAILTY
33	SHAUN OF THE DEAD
34	DOG SOLDIERS
35	THE MIST
36	DEAD END
37	THE SIGNAL
38	PONTYPOOL

39	*IDENTITY*
40	*THE EXORCISM OF EMILY ROSE*
41	*JENNIFER'S BODY*
42	*JOY RIDE*
43	*HOSTEL*
44	*JEEPERS CREEPERS*
45	*DISTURBIA*
46	*PLANET TERROR*
47	*THE HUMAN CENTIPEDE (FIRST SEQUENCE)*
48	*RESIDENT EVIL*
49	*SAW III*
50	*SAW IV*
51	*BATTLE ROYALE*
52	*BROTHERHOOD OF THE WOLF*
53	*PERFUME: THE STORY OF A MURDERER*
54	*FROM HELL*
55	*HARD CANDY*
56	*BEYOND RE-ANIMATOR*
57	*BOOK OF SHADOWS: BLAIR WITCH 2*
58	*THE FINAL DESTINATION*
59	*THE CONVENT*
60	*VAN HELSING*
61	*CUBE ZERO*
62	*CABIN FEVER 2: SPRING FEVER*
63	*BEHIND THE MASK: THE RISE OF LESLIE VERNON*
64	*GINGER SNAPS: UNLEASHED*
65	*STUCK*
66	*THE MUMMY RETURNS*
67	*THE BUTTERFLY EFFECT 2*

68	MY NAME IS BRUCE
69	CABIN FEVER
70	JASON X
71	EIGHT LEGGED FREAKS
72	TEETH
73	LESBIAN VAMPIRE KILLERS
74	BUBBA HO-TEP
75	JEEPERS CREEPERS II
76	SWEENEY TODD: THE DEMON BARBER OF FLEET STREET
77	SALEM'S LOT
78	THE DESCENT
79	HELLRAISER: INFERNO
80	THE TEXAS CHAINSAW MASSACRE
81	THE TEXAS CHAINSAW MASSACRE: THE BEGINNING
82	THE HITCHER
83	SILENT HILL
84	FEAST
85	REPO! THE GENETIC OPERA
86	THE ATTIC EXPEDITIONS
87	ROSE RED
88	THE DESCENT: PART 2
89	ABOMINABLE
90	VALENTINE
91	VACANCY
92	BLACK CHRISTMAS
93	P2
94	CHERRY FALLS
95	RED DRAGON
96	DOLAN'S CADILLAC

97	THE LAST HOUSE ON THE LEFT
98	MAY
99	SECRET WINDOW
100	SESSION 9
101	THE HOUSE OF THE DEVIL
102	KING KONG
103	SAW V
104	TIMECRIMES
105	28 DAYS LATER...
106	RESIDENT EVIL: APOCALYPSE
107	AVP: ALIEN VS. PREDATOR
108	JURASSIC PARK III
109	THE BOX
110	SAW VI
111	THE RING

#1
HANNIBAL

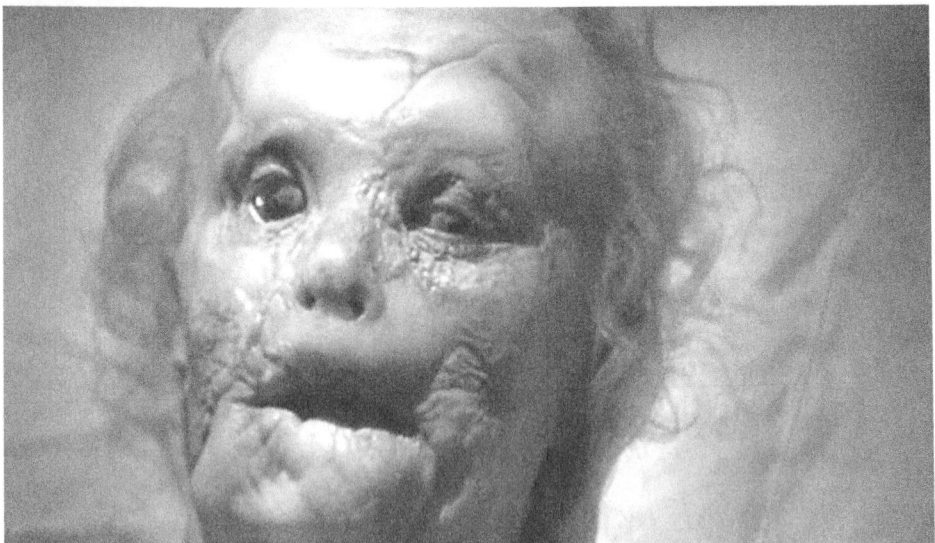

2001

A runaway cannibal is tracked down by the police and a past victim of his.

8/8

Anthony Hopkins approached the Hannibal persona with subtlety, class, vocabulary and calm in 1991's Silence of the Lambs. His passivity was concerning and he was frightening by implication only until the third act. He was a mysterious figure in the shadow of another; both a protagonist and an antagonist to Jodie Foster's character. She is replaced by Julianne Moore in this sequel.

Though her absence breaks an otherwise clean continuity; with references to the past and recognizable patterns, Moore fills the mandate with a fair rendition of Clarice Starling. This is Hopkins' show, regardless. The gore is glorified but celebrated by slow captivating build-up that pays off. The film is eerie, looks luxurious and the score gives significant gravitas to suspense.

It borrows from the cheesiest horror subgenres yet benefits from a good budget, stunning make-up, keen photography and the best actors money can rent. The end result is highly professional, calculated and always reaches full impact. Hannibal appears omniscient, as he always did, and his intelligence is terrifying when fully exposed. He is both who we follow and who we fear.

THE OTHERS

2001

The mother of two photosensitive children becomes convinced that her house is haunted.

8/8

This is the kind of film you want to watch in one streak, without interruption and in the right mood, because subsequent viewing won't be as impactful. A lot of this production resides in its surprises, scattered here and there, and in its twists. The Others will definitely become your go-to movie about ghosts for its quintessence and its haunting atmosphere.

Nicole Kidman deserves praise for her acting. She's not playing your run-of-the-mill mother. First, this is a period piece. Second, she's isolated in the middle of nowhere. Third, her husband is at war. Fourth, her kids are weird. There is more to this character than meets the eye. We know this because the first shot of the movie presents her in a state of panic. Her character never gets better.

Every word, in The Others, has a meaning. Alejandro Amenábar, writer, director and musician, shows you what he thinks you should see. His film is slow but surprisingly dense. The cast and sets are limited, but the film looks like a million bucks. It is visually rich, it is immersive and it's scary as hell. Also, all the actors, even the young ones, do a bang-up job.

#5
THE BUTTERFLY EFFECT

2004

A man afflicted by a supernatural disease learns to travel back in the past to make the present better.

7/8

The Butterfly Effect is a tragic supernatural thriller that deals with time travel in its own creative way using a logic we haven't seen before. Its main protagonist, Ashton Kutcher's character, uses passages from private journals he wrote to revisit his youth and alter the past to make the present better; better for him, his friend and his love interest.

The film deals with difficult subjects like pedophilia, violence, bad parenting, mental illness, physical disability, suffering and death. It is a story about regrets and remorse, of things we would've done differently had we known the consequences of our acts. Despite and implausible plot, this movie is extremely sad, very serious and highly introspective.

And, aside its complex concept, the script doesn't have major plot holes. For such a tragic story, it even has its fun moments. The writing is fine, the directing irreproachable, and the actors are so good they make us forget we're watching fiction. This movie passes by so fast it leaves us wanting more. The gimmick is poignant and strangely addicting.

#6
HOUSE OF WAX

2005

A group of teens stranded in a village near a strange wax museum realize their lives are in danger.

7/8

Elisha Cuthbert, Jared Padalecki, Paris Hilton, and Chad Michael Murray make this film epic, though it would still impress without them. They're not just talented actors, they remind us of people we know. They make this film fun and comfortable before it gets increasingly dark. This is the second time this story gets remade, and it is quite an enhancement. It's a slasher with an edge.

The writers know what a good movie is and that's exactly what they're giving us. They bank on common horror tropes, half the time, and somewhat re-invent them otherwise. The antagonists follow the same logic. We've seen their patterns before, but never quite like this. The budget is substantial, and the movie needs it to tell a big story. The set decoration and the special effects are massive.

Some of the pain inflicted is atrocious and, at times, hard to watch. The gore is brilliant. In regard to who bites the dust and in which order, the script does a pretty good job of keeping us guessing and on the edge of our seat. Personality flaws end up being assets. People we thought were protected by the writers get mutilated. You just can't take anything for granted. Great flick!

#7
DRAG ME TO HELL

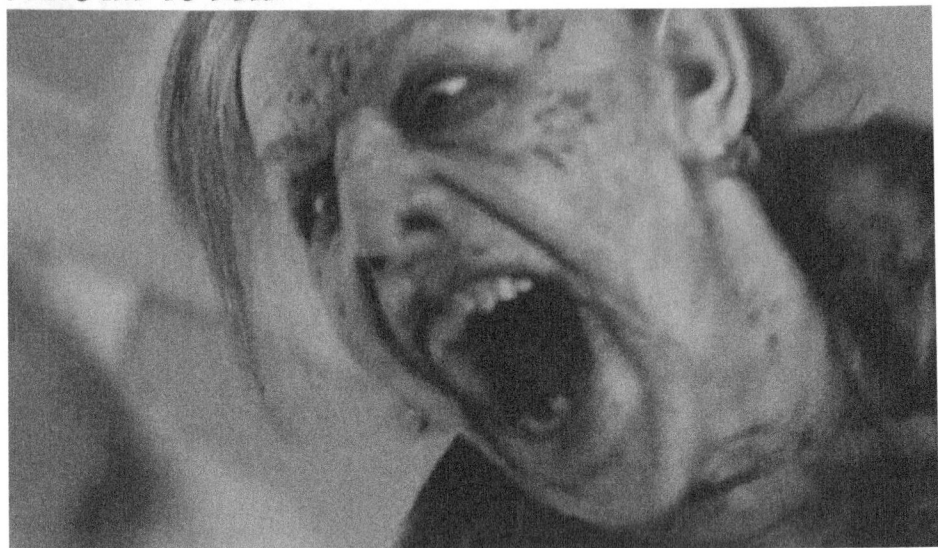

2009
A loan officer becomes the recipient of a supernatural curse.

7/8

When it comes to horror movies, Sam Raimi knows more than you do what's good for you. He pulls many tricks that he experimented with in the Evil Dead franchise. That is where he learned to build tension, make us laugh and frighten us, sometimes all at once. This is a very stressful film with excellent build-up, well-written characters and incessant terror.

The film is naturally paced, yet extremely calculated. When you're not scared, you're disgusted or feel terrible for Alison Lohman's adorable character. Witchcraft is a recurring theme. There is gore at every corner. The effects are 90% amazing and 10% made of bad CG. Who cares; this is one fun roller coaster ride that will make you laugh and jump just as much.

The jump scares are earned. The actors are irreproachable. The slapstick comedy gives Drag Me to Hell its signature. It wouldn't be half as interesting without it. Prepare to meet one of the most despicable and repulsive horror villains ever imagined. Sure, the story is kind of hard to keep up with and the ending is kind of weak, but most of this film is an absolute blast.

#10
HOLLOW MAN

2000

A scientist turned invisible by a newly discovered potion becomes a threat for his colleagues.

7/8

Watch Kevin Bacon lose his mind in ways only he can in a superior horror thriller directed by the great Paul Verhoeven. Elisabeth Shue plays the love interest and the protagonist. She is the ideal ex-girlfriend and a perfect fit for the role. Hollow Man is the classic story of a rushed scientific experiment gone wrong, but with a huge budget invested in big names and special effects.

In this unofficial remake of The Invisible Man, Bacon becomes increasingly unstable and violent. This is a remarkable thriller when it is tense, an excellent horror movie when it is violent and enthralling science fiction otherwise. The metamorphosis sequences are stellar. We get to see complex and somewhat realistic 3-D renders of the whole transformation from opacity to transparency and back.

The actors are on top of their game. The film wouldn't work without their chemistry. They make use believe in what they see despite the green screens and color keying. They have a plausible love and hate dynamic, a past and a present, conflicts and friendships. Despite the fantastic elements they deal with, their dialogue is mature and right out of a 90's titillating thriller. This is a must see!

WWW.TERROR.CA

#11
FINAL DESTINATION

2000

Death comes back at a medium who saved his classmates' life and his own after a premonition.

7/8

Final Destination's supernatural serial killer is slow, invisible, strategic and angry. It is an ill-defined force that answers to specific rules only talented writers could come up and juggle with. It's a character that doesn't need to be recast in sequels and therefore has the potential to generate an infinite franchise. It is a frightening villain because you can't kill it; let alone touch it.

The performances are authentic, energetic and supported by strong dialogue. In real life, "signs" are reserved for the crazy who see meaning in the smallest details and who connect dots where there are none. Devon Sawa's character is patronized for it, making him the default geek and some guy no one believes. While this is a recurring horror cliché, here it feels natural, logical, pertinent.

This is one of the smartest and most eccentric gimmicks of modern horror movie history. Imagine an intangible telekinetic force that slowly shapes events, mistakes and catastrophes to its advantage and aligns them in a way to assault the same person iteratively; making sure they are dead before dealing with the next victim. Other details are handled by a spoon-fed but entertaining procedural.

#12
FINAL DESTINATION 3

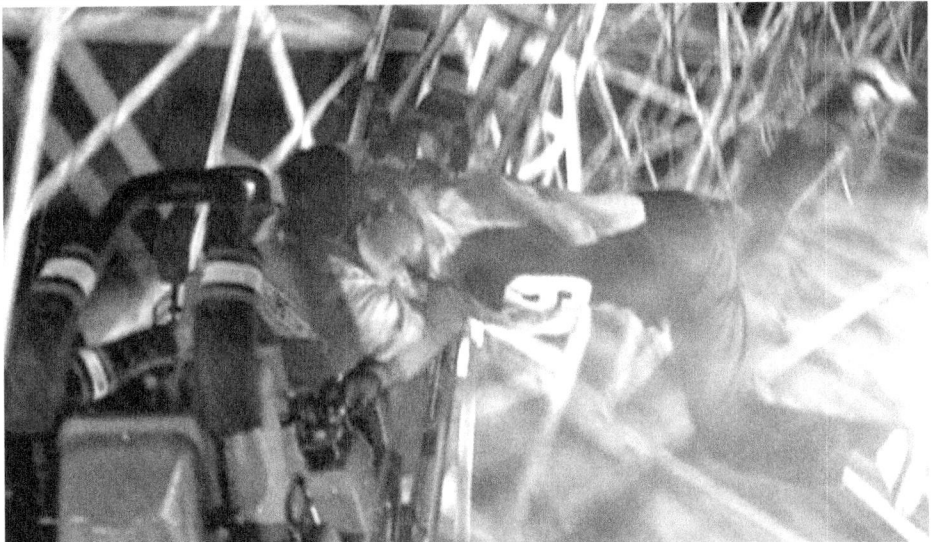

2006

Teenagers saved from a roller coaster incident by a psychic friend are stalked and killed by Death.

7/8

The tragic and over the top intro mayhem, here, takes place in a theme park and sets the tone for a carnivalesque sequel. The writers are getting more superficial, the effects more ambitious; though not always convincingly polished, and the actors are effervescent. The cast was renewed again, for better or worse, and assigned paper thin personas hard to bond with.

It's a little sexier, much dumber, immature, and it bends the gimmick's rules. Somewhat a copy/paste of the original film, Final Destination 3 eventually meets a dead end. Since Tony Todd, the only face we can attribute to the Reaper, isn't showing up, any hope for backstory is loss. There is no mystery left to explore. Continuity is from now on hindered and any attempt at a procedural is futile.

The kills are getting creative and edited in a way to feel parodically stretched. The gore is extreme, imaginative, and feels earned because build-up is well paced. This is still a high budget production but one that takes many shortcuts. We're losing layers, actors, characters, locations, and our connection to the original story; therefore getting a simpler, quintessential slasher in return.

WWW.TERROR.CA

#13
SAW II

2005

A SWAT team leader negotiates with a terminally ill murderer in attempt to save his son from a poison and a booby-trapped maze.

7/8

Jigsaw, the contraption serial killer, gathered a bunch of people in a condemned building and puts them to the test, again; this time as a group. Pushed to their limits, all characters eventually become hostile to each other. This is, in a way, Saw on a larger scale. The pace is faster, the cast larger, and the game more complex.

The story blends well with the first movie, some characters return and there is stunning continuity. The visual style and the filtered photo match the original picture. No plot detail is left to chance and every subplot finds its purpose. Expect the same score, excellent performances, significant production quality, the same frantic editing, and, of course, high shock and stress value.

Half of it takes place in Jigsaw's workshop, with a villain on the verge of death and with nothing to lose: someone that can't be threatened or reasoned with. He watches people die one by one in the most creative ways, something we now expect from the creators. The gimmick is simple: suffer or die suffering. It's not much of a choice, but it's terrifyingly relatable and horribly satisfying...

#14
FINAL DESTINATION 2

2003
People saved from a high way pile up by a medium are visited by Death.

7/8

Part 1 had a solid script supporting a great gimmick that left people wanting more; serial murders by an invisible force that can be slowed down or postponed but never destroyed. What's more, it was based on the premise that the main protagonist was implicitly psychic. Part 2 makes the most of these foundations and delivers more of what we liked the first time around.

Most sequels suffer from the fact that their lead is traumatized, which often gives the audience no party to crash. Final Destination 2 is sometimes more serious, sometimes lighter, introduces new characters and makes Ali Larter secondary. Devon Sawa is nowhere to be found. Tony Todd makes scary faces and says scary things again. Horror fans will geek on it as much as the mainstream audience.

We're here for the imaginative kills and we get a lot of it. It isn't as eerie and mysterious as the original, but it spares us a redundant procedural. It trades scares for action and vulnerability for resilience. By tradition, it starts with carnage and ends with carnage. In the middle is nothing but immature and stretched out suspenseful gore, courtesy of characters we don't really care about.

#15
DAWN OF THE DEAD

2004

Strangers take refuge in a mall during a zombie outbreak.

7/8

Those coming into this unaware of the classic horror movie it remakes will have their mind blown and will fully appreciate the ride regardless. This film stands alone but honors a great legacy. Hardcore fans of George A. Romero's work will recognize antisocial patterns of 1985's dramatic Day of the Dead transported in shopping mall sets reminiscent of 1978's more comedic Dawn of the Dead.

The zombies look amazing, but they run and twitch. Because our leads must survive a while for a movie to exist, the living dead are limited in number to compensate for their speed and strength. The only issue this creates, here, is that the mall isn't invaded, per say, until late in the story. It feels like a wasted gimmick at first, but the script wants to depict human conflicts instead.

Writer James Gunn is familiar with Romero's ways. He purposely isolates the victims; a powerful ensemble cast of popular names, from the zombies for most of the runtime to force them to survive creatively, in addition to dealing with the alienation, the infection, the claustrophobia and the paranoia. He knows that the living dead are simple villains that generate rhetorical story arcs.

#16
GINGER SNAPS

2000

A teenager bitten by a werewolf undergoes slow metamorphosis.

7/8

To be terrifying, a werewolf movie needs to have its protagonist be afflicted by the curse and not be mere victim of the beast itself. Apprehending the transformation represents half the fear there is to be had in this subgenre and Ginger Snaps is excellent at it. It offers a teenage but not cute girly spin on the typical formula and goes as far as metaphorizing puberty in the werewolf equation.

The use of 3-D animation isn't abusive and most of the good stuff relies on practical effects, fortunately. The visual are always frightening and lit just right, though more of the beast should have been shown. The film looks good but can't afford showing it all. It would rather redeem itself with a strong script and performances that win you over, given character development is your thing.

Werewolves were never this sexy. Katharine Isabelle is a violent and sexualized version of 1985's Teen Wolf's coming of age rendition; proof that times have changed. Humor, sensuality and horror find a perfect balance in the hands of Karen Walton and John Fawcett who flesh out a tragic monster evolving from protagonist to antagonist over a few days and who can titillate us as well as scare us.

WWW.TERROR.CA

#17
SCREAM 3

2000

A copycat killer decimates the cast and crew of a popular horror movie based on actual events.

7/8

Scream gets a little more grandiose, graciously moving its plot and its survivors to Hollywood. The main protagonists are adults, now, and they have been through a lot. The tone is consequentially dark, but spiced up by the re-introduction of stereotypical characters and surreal settings. The action mostly takes place on the set of a film inspired by the events of the two first Scream movies.

By tradition, the new faces are either used as slasher meat, red herrings or both. Guessing the killer's identity is harder than ever, the characters having been left underdeveloped and the amount of speaking roles having increased. Scream purists will find the script clustered, superficial, and cold when it comes to dialogue. This one isn't big on details and human chemistry.

The previous film was a self-referential sequel; the third one focuses on the rules of trilogies. The game, then, becomes to second-guess the outcome, based on our personal fandom knowledge or hints left by the franchise, so far. As stated in Scream 3, for better or worse, anything goes in this one. It won't rub everybody the right way, but it's still a brilliantly directed high-budget slasher.

#18
AMERICAN PSYCHO

2000
A wealthy investment banking executive grows increasingly insane.

7/8

American Psycho introduces a protagonist who is both charming and despicable. Through his thoughts and actions, we understand he is a sociopath who will stop at nothing to shape the world as he sees fit. He is on the brink of a psychosis and we watch him regress with delight. He has no respect for women and is obsessively competitive towards men. Here's a one-way ticket into his madness...

This is a satire on the late 1980s and its yuppies. It takes place in Manhattan in all its glory. Patrick Bateman, the lead, hangs out in trendy restaurants that serve meals so pretentious they seem out of a fairy tale. The movie is sexy, kinky, and features both male and female nudity. It also contains one of the most legendary threesomes in film history!

The structure is unusual. Bateman's antagonist, a detective, is a stress factor but isn't much of a threat. Consequences to his murders are somehow inexistent, it seems, and his true enemy is his insanity, as it turns out. The social commentary is strong, yet you could miss it if you're not looking deep enough. American Psycho is a mainstream jewel and an instant classic.

#19
THE HOLE

2001

Four teenagers uncover and explore the depths of a sealed underground bomb shelter.

7/8

The Hole is at times poignant, frustrating, disturbing, but there is more, here, than meets the eye. This is a legendary mindfuck. The story is simple enough, but it gets increasingly layered the deeper we get. Parallel to the main timeline is a psychiatric investigation. This leads to one of the most powerful twists in the history of horror films and it happens sooner than you'd think.

Things gets very sinister passed a certain point. The teenagers realize they are locked inside the bunker they were partying in. Claustrophobia ensues. All this happens while the main protagonist, played by Thora Birch shows her unrequited love for Mike, one of two jocks, played by Desmond Harrington. Keira Knightley plays the hot chick and Laurence Fox her fling. All four are exceptional!

We get a good understanding of who everybody is, and they all react appropriately through the obstacles ahead. They are not exactly stereotypes; they remind us of people we know. They remind us of us. This film has a great kick, but it particularly stands out because of how shocking it gets. The suspenseful score makes everything better, and what an immersive bomb shelter set!

#20
WILLARD

2003

A troubled man discovers he shares a psychic link with rats and uses them in a revenge plot.

7/8

This is the second screen adaptation of a novel by Stephen Gilbert. Every second of it is enchanting, thanks to a mystical trio composed of Crispin Glover, a creepy sociopath, his invasive and annoying mother, played by Jackie Burroughs, and R. Lee Ermey, a persecuting boss who's everything Willard despises and vice versa. All characters are polarized versions of who they were in the 1971 version.

Glover owns every scene he's in and is particularly good when he's alone or spending time with rats. He also has strong one on one arguments with R. Lee Ermey's character, who nobody should bother debating with. The film is not technically a comedy, but it has a sharp sense of humor. We're the only ones laughing, mind you, this is otherwise a dark experience.

The way Willard gains influence among rodents is presented interestingly. We get a nice montage that makes us buy what the script is selling, including a supernatural element we never really question that lasts until the very end of the film. With its mesmerizing score and its superior directing, Willard is a unique horror movie you'll want to put at the top of your watch list.

WWW.TERROR.CA

#21
FRAILTY

2001

A man confesses to an FBI agent that his father's visions led to a series of murders.

7/8

Fifteen minutes in, the hook is introduced. And there you have it, a father recruiting his kids in a demon hunt. He's having visions, so he's either psychotic or blessed by God. The difference between magic and mental illness is what everyone else sees. The father, played by Bill Paxton in one of his best roles, involves his two kids in his madness. The oldest one doesn't like it one bit...

The kids are played by young Matt O'Leary and Jeremy Sumpter. We instantly buy them as brothers. Adult Adam, one of them, is played by Matthew McConaughey, years later, who retells to an FBI agent what is pretty much a period piece to us. The main timeline takes place in 1979, when people still had simple lives; before the internet and satellite television. It's also when we stopped praying.

This is a brutal film, but the violence is not particularly graphic. A lot is accomplished through clever, tight editing. Sound effects account for a lot when it comes to implicit pain. Frailty is kind of slow, but well-paced. The suspense constantly rises until it reaches an amazing third act that you won't soon forget. This one will make you question your faith, or lack thereof...

#22
SHAUN OF THE DEAD

2004

A man attempts to gather his friends, his family and his girlfriend during a zombie invasion.

7/8

Shaun of the Dead is a story about a bunch of nobodies trying to survive a zombie invasion. It is, most will agree, one of the funniest zombie movie parodies out there. Not one joke falls flat. Have Simon Pegg and Nick Frost ever offered anything less than hilarity? These actors are legendary. Here, they play a dynamic duo who look like they've known each other all their lives.

Their characters are so dumb, and either drunk or hung over, that they never see the invasion coming and they become stuck with the repercussion very late in the game. They must save the day, and they're not very successful. The other actors do bang-up jobs, too, including the extras who play zombies with a slapstick behavior we haven't really seen before. The make-up can be persuasive, too.

The montages are very cool and always amusing. They punctuate the movie and give it a nice cadence. They constantly show strategies and, then, the reasons they failed or some retaliation. The editing is extremely dynamic and a comedic element in itself. If you haven't seen this yet, I'm probably not the first person to urge you to. This is part of the Cornetto Trilogy.

#23
DOG SOLDIERS

2002

A routine military exercise in the wilderness turns into a nightmare.

7/8

Werewolf movies are rarely just about werewolves. They often belong to one or several other subgenres, perhaps to tell a bigger story. Dog Soldier is no exception. It is the Predator and Night of the Living Dead rendition of a werewolf flick. It features British soldiers on a training mission. They're tough guys with guns stuck in the middle of the woods. This story pretty much writes itself.

The werewolves are bipeds. We see a lot of them but only in quick shots. They're scary and sure do a lot of damage. They're smart and organized, and aren't apparently allergic to silver. We get three transformation scenes and they're not impressive. They're cheats. That being said, there aren't many lycanthrope films out there, let alone good ones, and this is one of the best.

The actors are good but the characters are generic. They're soldiers, after all. The gore is disgustingly realistic. The film is cold and dark, but contains a healthy dose of humor to lighten things up from one action scene to another. The movie starts with a bang, slows down, but soon picks up the pace, escalates in a crescendo and never let's go. What a ride!

#24
THE MIST

2007

A mist unleashes bloodthirsty creatures on a small town, where a band of citizens hole up in a supermarket.

7/8

Frank Darabont, director and screenwriter, proves once again that he can adapt Stephen King's material like no one else. He can deliver, within budget, a stunning production quality. The actors are solid. The casting is excellent. Everybody fits their part. The action mainly takes place in one location; a grocery store, and the film is apparently shot on a sound stage. It's so claustrophobic!

The screenplay is ambitious. The creature design and most of the storyline could be described as Lovecraftian. The creatures' origin is and will remain a mystery. Their goal and motivations are never explained. As one of the character suggests, at some point, they are either supernatural, biblical or man-made. They could be anything. It's what makes them creepy. The mist itself is an enigma.

The 3D effects are a little too shiny for my taste, and that's the film's only flaw. As is often the case in apocalyptic movies, human's most resilient enemies are other humans. Religion and spirituality are crucial to the plot. Romance and family are important themes, too. The Mist is frightening, introspective, but it's also terribly sad. And what a great ending!

#25
DEAD END

2003

On Christmas Eve, on their way to a celebration, a family tries a shortcut and soon regrets it.

7/8

Dead End is as amusing as it is sinister. It's a Christmas-themed horror movie, but it couldn't be further from a celebration. It sends shivers down our spine on many occasions. It is suspenseful, it is sad, and it contains imaginative gore. The screenplay is clever and colorful. The film is told like a classic campfire tale. The budget is relatively small but that's never a problem.

Lin Shaye plays a mother who is losing grip on her family and, soon, on reality. Ray Wise is the abrupt and impatient husband and father, Mick Cain is the comic relief, Alexandra Holden the traumatized daughter and William Rosenfeld her boring boyfriend. These guys have great chemistry. We totally buy them as a family. When shit hits the fan, we sympathize instantly.

Most of the running time is spent inside and around a car, at night, and this probably wasn't easy to shoot. This movie being dialogue-driven, we're in good hands with writers and directors Jean-Baptiste Andrea and Fabrice Canepa. The actors deliver their lines effortlessly. It rolls off their tongues. The creators truly caught lightning in a bottle with Dead End.

#26
THE SIGNAL

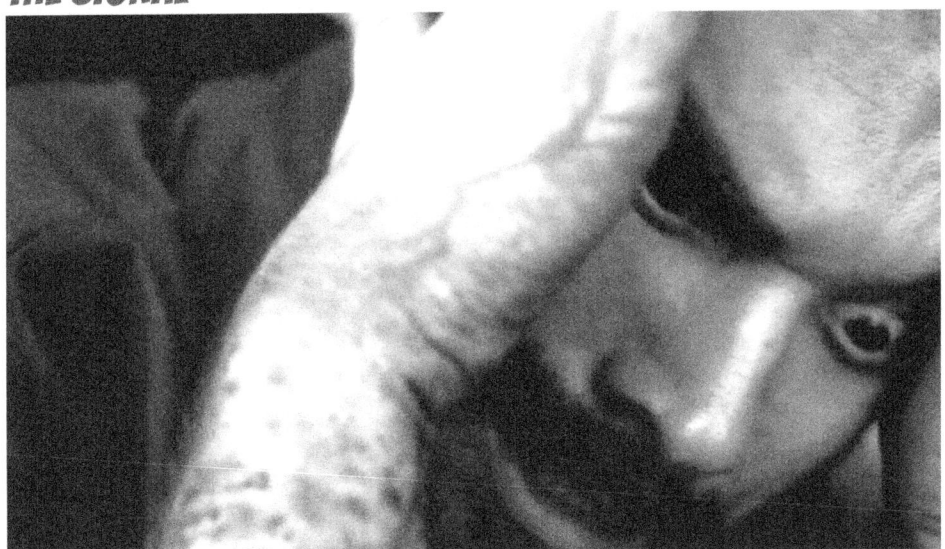

2007

A mysterious electronic transmission turns people into killers.

7/8

The Signal is told in three parts with a non-linear structure; each written and directed by their own filmmaker. The segments all blend together seamlessly. This apocalyptic scenario is, ironically, much more plausible yet imaginative than a zombie outbreak, presented as it is. We're talking contagious psychosis and mass hysteria caused by static frequencies.

This mindfuck will take you to such extremities that you might end up laughing and shivering at the same time. It is so sensational that it will probably stick with you long after it's over. It is melancholic, sick and twisted, and then some. The humor is on and off, and it acts as an accelerant to the shock factor. The film is extremely gory and no character gets spared when it comes to violence.

The middle segment is the most interesting one. It uses creative ways to take actors in and out of the frame to interchange them, and therefore to simulate everyone's hallucinations. We can't tell if special effects or compositing are involved, or if the actors and the camera are perfectly synchronized instead, but we know this isn't a big budget production and we never question what we see.

#27
PONTYPOOL

2008

A radio host interprets the possible outbreak of a deadly virus contracted vocally.

7/8

Radio stations are such an atmospheric place to set horror movies. They're isolated, small spaces, and they require a limited cast. Radio hosts are often the first to learn about disasters and other incidents, and they warn the population about potential danger. Radio stations, ironically, are not protected from invasions by zombies and other contagious creatures.

We've got three talented leads. Stephen McHattie gives the most memorable performance as the news anchor. He has a witty sense of humor and gets the best lines. He's a little eccentric and somewhat self-centered. The relationship between him and his colleagues is particular. There's his ex and his assistant. We instantly buy their unusual chemistry.

The dialogue gets increasingly hypnotic, as the story unfolds. We're dealing with a disease that spreads vocally. That concept, in itself, is extremely imaginative. The fact that we absorb most of the explanation shows proficient writing. Our mind is constantly fucked with, but we always have an understanding of what the characters are going through. Lightning in a bottle!

#28
IDENTITY

2003

Stranded at a desolate motel during a rain-storm, a group of strangers start dying one by one.

7/8

Two things make Identity a marvel. First, it has one of the best twists in film history. You won't see it coming. Second, it has an incredible ensemble cast. We're talking John Cusack, Ray Liotta, Amanda Peet, John Hawkes, Alfred Molina, Clea DuVall, Jake Busey and Rebecca De Mornay. How can you go wrong with a team like that? How is this casting even possible?

The film is very dynamic, unpredictable, sporadically gory, tense, scary and a little bit sad. We go through a wide range of emotions in a short period of time. In a nutshell, it is inspired by Ten Little Indians. You can say this, of course, of every whodunit, but it's especially true here. Identity has a surreal aspect to it, and it doesn't exclude the possibility of a supernatural element.

Trying to guess who the killer is can be frustrating. The creators just won't give that away easily. Have fun guessing, but you'll probably fail. There are so many layers to Identity that it's worth watching over and over. Several clues are dropped and you'll probably miss them all. This is, simply put, one of the best psychological thrillers of its decade.

#29
THE EXORCISM OF EMILY ROSE

2005

A lawyer takes on a homicide case involving a priest who performed an exorcism on a girl.

7/8

1973's The Exorcist set the bar pretty high in terms of possession movies. Perhaps the goal was never to beat the classic, but, rather, to address exorcism differently. The Exorcism of Emily Rose is a trial film and a legal procedural with a strong religious layer. These subgenres don't often collide and the end result, in this case, is enthralling.

This film reaches its full potential on several occasions, when the calm and the slow pacing of the procedural are sporadically interrupted by loud and frightening sequences of possession. We're constantly caught off-guard. So, is Emily epileptic, psychotic or downright possessed? You'll find out soon enough. Emily's hallucinations are terrifying, and her contortions are petrifying.

Although all actors do a bang-up job, Jennifer Carpenter is killing it. While this story isn't all about her, and despite the fact that her scenes are in fact flashbacks, she's the center of attention. The writers feel they need to punctuate Laura Linney's character's life with demonic manifestations, and those sometimes feel forced, often meeting a dead end. It is the script's only major flaw.

#30
JENNIFER'S BODY

2009

A possessed high school cheerleader turns into a succubus.

7/8

This movie falsely attempts to glorify Megan Fox's beauty. In fact, as it turns out, Amanda Seyfried outcutes her. She has more depth, she's the girl next door, and, despite the film's title, this is her movie, not Fox's. The girls share a powerful bond. Lesbianism is addressed, but that's not where the focus is. In Jennifer's Body, Fox's character dies and comes back as a succubus.

What makes the picture so exciting is that the exposition happens before and after the inciting incident. When we're not watching a band play in a bar, we're spending time at school, at a dance or in suburbia. The creators really went for a cheerful vibe and familiar circumstances. The story is somewhat anachronic. If at first the plot seems illogical, know that it will eventually add up.

The acting is stellar. The characters completely immerse us. The soundtrack is fun. It's pretty much one song and it's made fun of repeatedly. If Seyfried's character wasn't so cynical, this movie would be at times touching. She ruins any attempt at romance. The film is scary, sexy, but also extremely funny when it turns into a comedy. Jennifer's Body is time well spent. It needs to be seen.

#31
JOY RIDE

2001

A truck driver torments two brothers who pranked him.

7/8

Joy Ride is, without a doubt, one of the best road movies out there. It is flawlessly written and transposed to screen by the keen eyes of experienced cinematographers. It lengthily exposes three likable protagonists played by Steve Zahn, Paul Walker and Leelee Sobieski. Their performance is authentic and layered. They are the boys and girls next door.

J.J.Abrams and Clay Tarver lay out a simple synopsis and stick to it; the way old films used to. It's a horror film so it gets tempted by the supernatural but prefers the subtlety of surrealism. It is a perfect companion piece to 1971's Duel and 1986's The Hitcher. This peculiar formula has been tested before and never gets tired, given the ambiance is dense enough and the suspense well executed.

This movie succeeds on those levels. What's more, a road movie typically involves car chases and stunts which this one pulls off incredibly well. The killer's truck looks mean; filmed with calculated framing and movement and in angles meant to scare and alienate. Even the action scenes are darker than heroic. As a bonus, horror movie fans get a new marketable horror villain called "Rusty Nail".

#32
HOSTEL

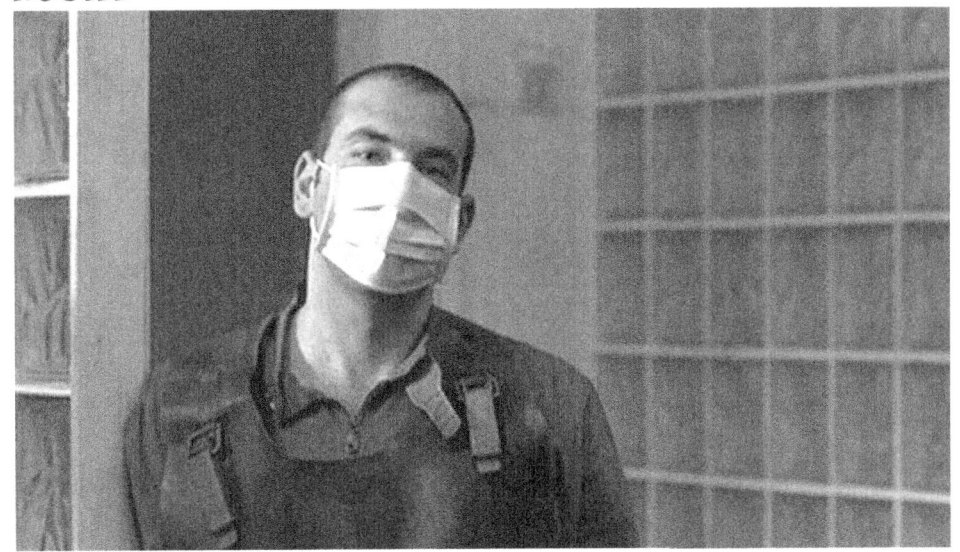

2005

Three friends travel to Slovakia to party and have sex but find danger instead.

7/8

On the surface, Hostel is a thriller about friends backpacking far, in a distant region, where they eventually get in big trouble. A good amount of time is spent exposing the main characters, making them people we'd love to know and would rather not see suffer when the main threat hits them. This film contains exhaustive character exposition, but gory torture is its main attraction.

You can call Hostel misogynist and xenophobic; the truth is it strikes where it hurts and it's usually what horror movies strive to do. It's highly exploitative, it's scary, and it's supported by great sets that sometimes inspire freedom, sometimes terror. It plays on our fear of the unknown but by stripping away all potential surrealism and keeping it real. This is as visceral as horror gets...

The film piggy backs on our fear of racism, terrorism and wars. The special effects are built to make the audience cringe and, to that effect, near perfection. Even considering many small parts necessitated the local casting of actors who can't speak English, the dialogue generally comes out as authentic. Hostel will shock many but, in the end, deserves to be called a classic.

#33
JEEPERS CREEPERS

2001

Siblings driving home from Spring break stumble upon a murderer's hideout.

7/8

The Creeper, new horror icon, remains an enigma to us and to the protagonists for the majority of the plot and then beyond. What starts like a typical road horror movie in the likes of Joy Ride, released the same year, becomes something unexpected and barely foreshadowed in the second half. In fact, this unusually paced slasher flick hides another familiar subgenre.

This film is accessible to the mainstream horror crowd but ventures in controversial zones. The villain poses multiple threats and instigates somewhat safe scares, but the depth of his perversion is what makes him both memorable and terrifying. He is, in a way, a glorified rapist. He is most admirable for his mythos, his M.O., and the fact that he comes with his own song.

Jeepers Creepers rekindles horror movie ideas and imagery we hadn't seen in years. Some concepts, here, are reminiscent of ideas considered burnt long ago and find a new audience in the hands of Victor Salva, writer and director. All planets deliberately align for a sequel, and therefore a franchise, from the first scenes in but the film manages to tell a story that feels complete regardless.

#34
DISTURBIA

2007

A teenager living under house arrest becomes convinced his neighbor is a serial killer.

7/8

Disturbia is reminiscent of Rear Window and Fright Night, but it's its own thing. The story is simple, and we've seen it countless time, but it was never told so lightly and with such an innocent tone. An interesting relationship evolves harmoniously between the three main protagonists. Two of them become romantically linked. The third wheel becomes the comic relief.

As a classic psychological thriller, the film hits every checkbox on the list. It's one of the best of its type. It is a quintessential thriller. It is intuitive. It flows admirably. It's predictable and, sometimes, predictable is fine. The performances are remarkable. Shia LaBeouf and David Morse are particularly good. Carrie-Anne Moss underplays.

Disturbia is brilliantly written and perfectly orchestrated to give us one hell of a ride. It has a lot of exposition, and that's not a problem. Part of the exposition involves a cute romantic arc that isn't realistic, very improbable, yet infinitely touching. Psychological thrillers are becoming a rarity but there is room for more and Disturbia proves it.

#35
PLANET TERROR

2007

A bio-weapon is released and turns thousands into zombies.

7/8

Planet Terror is released as a double feature with Quentin Tarantino's Death Proof and pays homage to exploitation flicks of the 1970s. It is an unusual zombie story with exceptional protagonists. There is the hypochondriac doctor, the nurse with a syringe fetish, the stripper with a riffle for a leg, the acrobat outlaw who fights with knives and the butcher who protects his secret sauce.

The screen is altered with a dust and scratch film filter that brings us back in time, but this is shot in digital. You'll rarely see horror with such realistic gore. Planet Terror is a drama with intelligent humor. Some of the protagonists are bad guys with baggage, so there are initial conflicts. The zombies aren't exactly simple either. They don't appear brain dead, which is interesting.

With its catchy score, its imaginative practical effects, its extreme digital compositing, its impressive stunts and its multiple explosions, Planet Terror is way above your average zombie film. In fact, the undead are just a pretext for great characters to evolve and die in gruesome ways. Planet Terror has an amazing cast of tough men and strong, sexy women. Most actors are big names.

#36
THE HUMAN CENTIPEDE (FIRST SEQUENCE)

2009

A mad doctor kidnaps and stitches together three tourists from anus to mouth.

7/8

There are few things worse than a car breakdown leading you under a psychopath's scalpel blade. Getting stitched buttock to mouth to your best friend and to a stranger by the hand of a mad surgeon is one of them. Rarely has torture porn used such a strong gimmick. The synopsis alone inspires fear and disgust. The Human Centipede is downright traumatizing and may make you sick.

Aside from some frustratingly improbable subplots, and despite the surreal premise, you buy what you see on screen. It's well shot and not as cheesy as one might think. There is pretty much a single location and a small amount of well fleshed characters. This setup allows for confined build-up that culminates into an amazing claustrophobic carnage so intense some might feel like pausing the film.

You will not want to eat before, during or after watching, and it will mark you for weeks. The disgusting stuff is mostly implicit and the gore limited, yet we feel the pain. It builds tension masterfully, makes you fear the worst, gives you even worse than implied, mixes humiliation, kink, sadism, fetishism, even. It's one sick movie, but it hits all the notes the ideal horror movie should.

#37
RESIDENT EVIL

2002

A military unit explores a zombie infested maze controlled by a super computer.

7/8

Though it doesn't exactly reflect the video game that it is based on, Resident Evil legitimately feels like one. Its characters are emotionally strong, agile and armed to the teeth. Many are throw-away and the ones we are mainly centering on are amnesic. They are stuck in a maze where they succumb to death one after another in mind-boggling ways; some by zombie bite, some by machines.

The composited zombies could use additional passes, but every other aspect of the aesthetic is spot on. The camera is always where it should be and sometimes beyond. Even seemingly useless close-ups end up revealing hints crucial to the plot. Every frame is studied and the photography is impeccable. We toggle between action and horror with ease, either cheering for the heroes or fearing for them.

At times, the science-fiction facets somewhat saturate the screenplay. Resident Evil is also an adventure film in which the protagonists always move forward without looking back. The story takes place inside a secret laboratory filled with traps, so, as opposed to the original game, we get much more depth than a mere haunted house packed with flesh-eating creatures.

#38
SAW III

2006

Threatened by a deadly contraption, a doctor must perform brain surgery on her dying captor.

7/8

Two stories are being told at once. We follow both a surgeon who's forced to save the villain's life and a man stuck in an improvised labyrinth whose backstory is unclear. By now, we know we're in for gore and crazy twists. The two previous narrative structures were more intricately crafted, but this is by no mean a weak sequel. It certainly doesn't hold back.

The film's biggest weakness is that it pushes the creativity so far that it loses the shocking plausibility of the previous films. We're increasingly asked to suspend disbelief. The writing is still smart; just not its usual self. The horror, in this franchise, has been emanating from a clever, horrifying mix of dilemmas and schemes set up by an evil genius. This element is stronger than ever.

The torture devices are more aesthetic; not the ones that necessarily rip you apart. The editing is sometimes abusive, but then it also keeps things quick, with minimal dialogue and little filler. Continuity is remarkable. Even when considering the artistic liberties taken, this one is as homogeneous as the first sequel was; so much so that the series is slowly starting to feel like one big movie.

WWW.TERROR.CA

#39
SAW IV

2007

A detective has ninety minutes to solve a dangerous puzzle and save his colleague.

7/8

With Jigsaw now dead, we are left with a bunch of people trying to survive the games he left behind, manipulated by the thought of imminent death. How can the franchise survive the loss of its icon? That's what flashbacks are for. Because this was the intended direction, it comes as a strength more than a plot hole that requires patching. It allows us to cover clues left behind, for one thing.

Saw's typical narrative plays with perceptions of time and space to pull its crazy twists, yet, even at this point, they remain hard to predict. For the first time, we don't feel limited to one location. The cast is enlarging too. Aside from sporadic protagonist exposition, old characters return or get a backstory. This is one for the fans. It's filled with subtle references and Easter eggs.

We investigate Jigsaw's past and that of his followers and family; his relationship with his first victims and his wife in regards to his secret scheme, namely. Expect the same optimal quality and the excellent acting as the previous films, but a somewhat faster pacing. The transitions are stunningly creative in this one and use little CG. The same can be said about the traps and torture props.

#40
BATTLE ROYALE

2000

The Japanese government secludes ninth-graders on a deserted island and forces them to kill each other.

7/8

Battle Royale's premise is ludicrous but memorable for the same reasons. It is a troubling drama interlaced with heartbreaking romance. At the core is an all-out war that can't end well. The film is tense from the first scenes in and foreshadows shocking events: students; friends and enemies, are forced to kill each other using randomly assigned weapons.

Two "wild cards" are thrown in the mix: a returning contestant and a psychopathic volunteer. They are battle-ready and they steal the show, casting a shadow on lesser characters. The weaker moments are highly philosophical and often anticlimactic, which might rub some viewers the wrong way. Fortunately, the action scenes compensate for the few weaker ones.

The island is gorgeous and filmed just right. It is made of beautiful plateaus, mountains and shores that would feel dreamy in a different film. The sadistic game's design makes good use of the environment and we get a good sense of geography. There are many characters for the script to manage so the pacing gets wobbly, but Battle Royale mostly keeps us biting our nails at the edge of our seats.

#41
BROTHERHOOD OF THE WOLF

2001

In 18th century France, a knight and naturist is asked to investigate the killings of hundreds by a mysterious beast.

7/8

You watch this film the way you drink old wine. It is bitter, it requires patience, but it's an experience. The first hour is extremely slow. This script is fluffy, political, padded and dialogue-heavy, but it all pays off. The second half is a pure delight. No trailer can do this film justice. It belongs to many genres and makes us go through a variety of emotions.

A lot of this is shot in a castle and in vast landscapes. Even the exterior shots are elegant. This is the kind of set design that makes you forget you're watching a movie. The exposition is extremely dense, for better or worse. The martial art sequences are breath-taking, but the slow motion is excessive. The beast is impressive but it's the only thing in the whole movie that looks fake.

The film is loosely based on a real-life series of killings that took place in France in the 18th century and the famous legend of the Beast of Gévaudan. Someone had to make a movie about it and they nailed it. They added romance, cool bad guys and extensive mythos. The creators are generous when it comes to providing mythos, in fact. They don't have to, but they do so and they do it brilliantly.

#42
PERFUME: THE STORY OF A MURDERER

2006

Born with a superior olfactory sense, a man attempts to create the world's finest perfume.

7/8

Perfume: The Story of a Murderer is a German period crime thriller. The screenplay is based on Patrick Süskind's 1985 novel Perfume about the sense of smell and its emotional impact. It is narrated, almost from beginning to end, by an unidentified voice. The film is so skillfully made that we can almost smell stench and the various perfumes presented to us.

As poetic and magical as Perfume is, it is, as the title indicates, the story of a serial killer. There are two dominant elements at play, here; Grenouille's supernatural power and his obsession for women. Dead women. In fact, he needs them dead to preserve their essence because there's no way they will cooperate through "enfleurage", his sinister extraction process.

The score is as ambitious as the photo and pretty much every aspect of this film. If you don't like Perfume, it just isn't for you. It's certainly not flawed. It is highly immersive and downright intoxicating; it's a trip inside the mind of a psychopath who we somehow relate to until we no longer can. The closer he gets to his goal, the more he loses our sympathy, until a memorable last act.

WWW.TERROR.CA

#43
FROM HELL

2001

In 1888, a police detective with psychic abilities investigates the murders of several prostitutes.

7/8

From Hell is a romanticized theory of Jack the Ripper's modus operandi and true identity. It is lavish, from its backdrop to its wardrobe. It's a slow and old-fashioned production, and it's oddly paced. Now, the film doesn't protect its twist as well as it could, which allows the extra half-hour to go places the typical Hollywood picture doesn't. The antagonist is probably not who you imagine.

Johnny Depp plays a clairvoyant police detective in Victorian-era London. In fact, we don't get confirmation he's a medium. Not initially. The man is addicted to opium and absinthe. Whether this helps him solve this case is part of the intrigue. Heather Graham plays a prostitute. She's great as always. She gives depth to a woman with none. She is the love interest.

The last act makes or breaks this story, depending on what you're ready to accept and what expectations you have. Ultimately, this is one of the best insights on serial killing. Jack the Ripper is among the first of his kind recorded in history, which gives him a mystical aura. But what if things weren't as we imagine? What if the truth was tangled? What if we looked in the wrong places?

#44
HARD CANDY

2005

A teenage girl attempts to expose a man under suspicion that he is a pedophile.

7/8

We center on two abnormal characters played by Patrick Wilson and Ellen Page. They are in the same room 95% of the running time. One is a photographer; the other a seemingly normal teenage girl. The film is dialogue-oriented and almost always framed in close-ups. The characters are both protagonists and antagonists, alternately or at the same time. Here's why...

Hard Candy is a horror thriller about underage sexuality and pornography. As a thriller, it explores the problematic from different angles while keeping the characters, their motivations and their background mysterious. As a horror movie, it pushes the boundaries of what you would expect from all the foreshadowing, and that includes a giant surprise at the halfway mark.

Both are impostors, both are seducers and both have a dark side. These are difficult characters to play and we, the audience, are stuck somewhere between them, scratching our heads, considering and reconsidering, at different times, as the story unravels. Hard Candy is minimalist and calculated. It plays with our minds and makes us question certain taboos rarely addressed in cinema.

WWW.TERROR.CA

#45
BEYOND RE-ANIMATOR

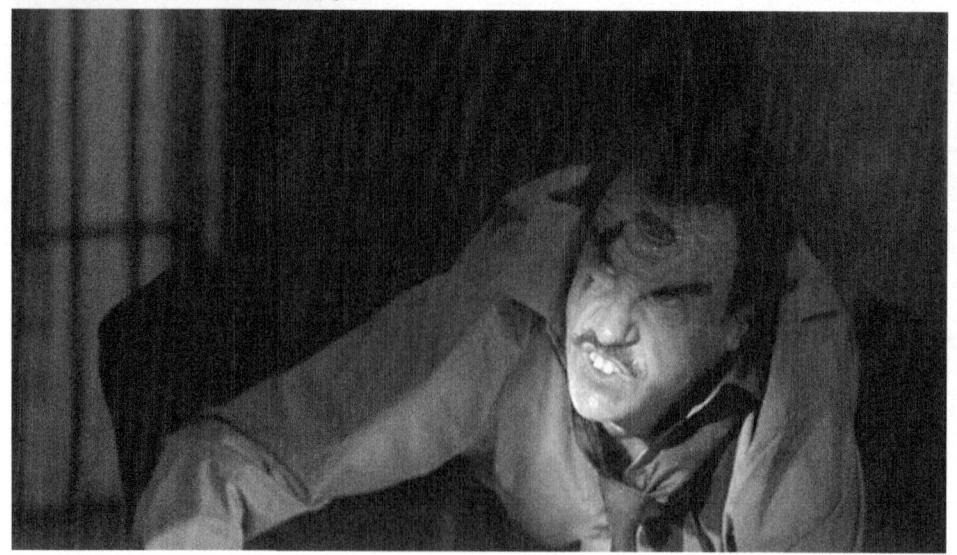

2003

A scientist who discovered how to reanimate the dead is sent to prison where he resumes his experiments.

6/8

Herbert West's acolyte from the two previous movies is not returning. Another smart and vulnerable protagonist is introduced and he does an okay job at filling the void. It marks the end of a classic mad scientist duo but establishes a similar relationship. Dr. Carl Hill is not making an appearance either, but is matched by the twisted warden's eccentric persona and sick mind.

Beyond Re-Animator is both gory and funny. The actors do an excellent job. The cinematography is arguably the best it's been and the production doesn't look cheap, adjusting well to digital. The writing is up to par and the film never gets boring. There is always something gruesome being talked about, eluded to or fully shown, and always with tongue in cheek in an attempt to uphold the tradition.

The script makes the global storyline progress rather than remake itself. After all, the source material has such great potential. It still treats its main protagonists as good guys, though West is rightfully sentenced to death and therefore confined for the whole running time. We manage to forgive him for his evil acts, disregarding his murder rate simply because his character is so hilarious.

#46
BOOK OF SHADOWS: BLAIR WITCH 2

2000

Haunted tour participants awaken a supernatural entity while partying in the woods.

6/8

The Blair Witch Project; previous installment, relied on a gimmick so strong that the makers of Part 2 avoided it altogether. In fact, they often allude to it and make it an integral part of the plot but do not use it as a form of editing. Part 1 popularized the "found footage" genre by lying to its audience and was very good at it. Part 2 is more traditional but still worth a watch.

The actors are no longer playing pretend and improvising but their performances allow for great build-up despite sometimes obscured storytelling. Blair Witch 2 stirs up the same fear amalgams Blair Witch 1 did and proves that the original script doesn't only rely on opportunistic viral marketing. We get another terrifying mind-fuck depicting threats that cannot be taken down with weapons.

This is a well written and directed movie that didn't get the care it deserved in the cutting room. The compositing is excessive in places and comes out as more of a nuisance than a clever way to tell a scary tale. The layered narrative isn't needed. Some might hate this sequel as a complement to a game changer in the film industry, but as a stand-alone haunting story it hits all the right notes.

#47
THE FINAL DESTINATION

2009

A racing car accident prevented by an omen saves lives and angers Death.

6/8

It has the weakest cast and the least interesting introduction mayhem in the franchise to date. Most survivors of the initial incident are aggressive, pessimist, annoying or heavily mourning someone's death. Globally, they end up bringing down a movie with more entertainment potential. The rest plays out how you'd expect, but this is the worst and laziest installment so far otherwise.

The movie was released in 3-D theaters. It is the perfect excuse for random gore to be thrown at the viewer; making us both duck and cringe, then laugh. This, of course, ends up breaking the fourth wall and doesn't work as well for the domestic audience. The CG looks cartoonish, but we're in Road Runner territory anyway; now that fright was generally replaced by black humor.

Some actors pull it off, but most of them are a major turn off. They aren't the compelling and layered bunch we had in Part 1 & 2. All Final Destination movies had something new to bring to the table and to add to the gimmick. This one is creatively dry, sadly. Expect more of the same but less of it in the end. It's still a great source of mindless fun, but it's not up to par.

#48
THE CONVENT

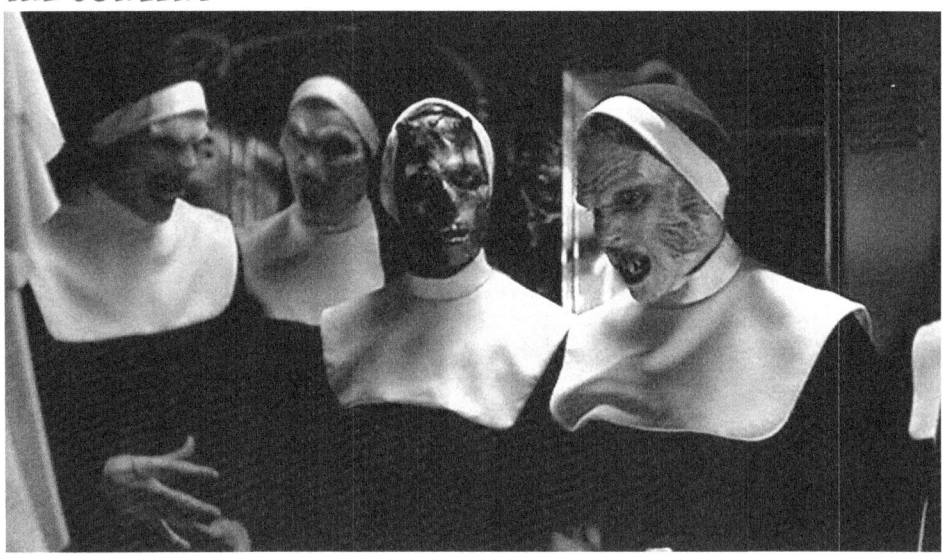

2000

A group of college students break into an abandoned convent and awaken demons.

6/8

The Convent's ensemble cast is vibrant, intoxicating and hilarious. Richard Trapp is hysterically funny as Frijole. He and Megahn Perry have some of the best lines in the movie. The scenes they share are golden. Saul and Dickie Boy, respectively played by David Gunn and Kelly Mantle, are the cherry on top. This is pretty much a comedic version of Night of the Demons.

There is an innocence to this film that really grows on you. It's an ambitious low budget production made by talented people devoted to make us piss our pants. The dialogue is colorful and peculiar for such a light-hearted horror comedy. It is witty, arrogant and whatever it needs to be. The last act is kind of weak. It feels rushed and is anticlimactic, the fun characters being long gone...

There were probably struggles in the editing room, because the post-production effects aren't all that. Other than that, director Mike Mendez and writer Chaton Anderson have a solid little movie on their hands. You'll remember it long after the credits roll. You'll remember the shroom trip, the fake Satanists and a hoard of angry twitching demons with neon paint all over their faces.

WWW.TERROR.CA

#49
VAN HELSING

2004

A beast hunter is caught in a war between good and evil.

6/8

This outstanding production by an expert in the paranormal adventure mixed subgenre, Stephen Sommers, unites all the classic monsters and gives them a steampunk edge. Dracula, his brides, Frankenstein, his monster, Igor, Mr. Hyde, werewolves, to name a few, are at war, here; a war between good and evil that Van Helsing, beast hunter, is stuck in the middle of.

If you accept 3-D characters, a glossy polish, and if this kind of epic rubs you the right way, then it will be the perfect film and you will be mesmerized. Otherwise, like most of us, you might still enjoy it but find it too lengthy. Van Helsing is a perpetual roller coaster ride punctuated with short dialogue, romance, humor and whatever helps us catch our breath.

This script is ambitious. The actors give superior performances and deserve a medal for coping with so many effects. We're, at all times, submerged in a romanticized dimension. Not much, here, happens in the real world. In fact, this is a world of color keying and fake sets. Van Helsing comes fully equipped with weapons and gadgets that couldn't possibly exist when this film takes places.

#50
CUBE ZERO

2004

A prison operator infiltrates the rigged labyrinth he controls to save a victim.

6/8

The little backstory and the few answers Cube 2: Hypercube provided led us to believe humans; possibly government officers, were nothing more than suited scientists of the future doing cervical experiments. Some might have felt Part 2 revealed too much and undershot the enigma. Cube: Zero, presumably a prequel, takes place in the rusty rooms and around the traps of a three-dimensional prototype.

What's more, evil is given at least four faces. Two of them are compelling protagonists who set a fun tongue-in-cheek tone. They are the better part of the backstory we get; other bits going as far as imaging life outside the cube that should have ended up on the cutting room floor. We are fed too much detail about the fact this this one takes place in the future and in our world.

We care little for the people inside the maze since we already know how their story goes and ends. Zachary Bennett plays Eric, the most interesting and strongest character in the franchise. He is who we worry about. His arc is immense and his perspective on the mystery makes him the perfect protagonist of a smart, well-written sequel. Part 1 was great, Part 2 was good and Part 0 is a blast!

#51
CABIN FEVER 2: SPRING FEVER

2009

A bottling factory unknowingly supplies a batch of contaminated water to a high school before prom night.

6/8

A frame-by-frame 2-D cartoon zip us through miles of unnecessary explanations, during the introduction credits, in regards to the plague's prolificity. No longer confined to a specific area, it spreads to the city; a high school, in this case, right before prom. Although some students are relatable, you can't worry about anyone's death, here. They all seem well-aware of their own tragic destiny.

Cabin Fever had humans as threat, and this was probably too much in the same film. The main gimmick is strong enough and this sequel knows it. It learns from the unmarketable aspects of the original and offers us a mainstream story that doesn't feel like every other one. It is cheesy, disgusting, but the story unveils more naturally because it embraces comedy.

Between the blood, pus, sperm and vomit hides tender tongue-in-cheek romance and easy satire. It's a smart movie purposely dumbed down and tinkered with in post-production but not for a dumb audience. It's namely an homage to prom night themed horror films of the 70's and 80's but delivered as a contamination flick. Entertaining from beginning to end, this is a no-brainer but a must-see!

#52
BEHIND THE MASK: THE RISE OF LESLIE VERNON

2006

Three filmmakers document a serial killer's routine.

6/8

When it comes to homages and parodies of slasher films, there is Scream and then there's Behind the Mask. The two brands are very entertaining and have nothing in common. The faux-documentary approach of Behind the Mask really grows on you. It's not what you would call a found footage movie, because, every so often, the creators use conventional film language to tell the story.

There are Easter eggs and cameos in the first act. The film mostly spoofs Halloween, Nightmare on Elm Street and Friday the 13th. It's fun to see the killer justify slasher tropes; stereotypes, body count, the obsession for virgins and final girls, doing a bad job of convincing us that this somehow makes sense. The filmmakers manage to keep us on the edge of our seat all along.

Behind the Mask doesn't just make fun of horror villains, it creates a new one. It's about the members of family who do not only kill but also learned to fake their death. Leslie Vernon always has a trick up his sleeve to escape death and lure his victims; sleigh of hands, illusion, scare tactics, and the list goes on. This is definitely one for the horror fans. This movie deserves a sequel!

#53
GINGER SNAPS: UNLEASHED

2004

Forced into rehab, a lycanthropic teenager struggles to postpone her metamorphosis.

6/8

Now Ginger is dead and the franchise is stuck with an obsolete hindering pun in its title. It picks up not far from where we left off with her sister and true protagonist Brigitte, played once more by Emily Perkins. Ginger is now the hybrid of a ghost and a vision, something that felt new in 1981's An American Werewolf in London but that feels shoehorned in, here.

Most of the story takes place within the walls of a psychiatric hospital that confines Brigitte beyond her affliction. She's considered a junkie and kept away from her antidote. This sets the table for a suspense and build-up more intense than Part 1's. The sequel is generally pessimist and much darker, though good support actors take care of brightening the mood.

The female characters are stronger and more interesting than their male counterpart; something noticeable in both films and a good way to stand out in a sea of generic horror. Like the first film, it is an hour-long transformation sequence that only delivers a fully developed werewolf during its last act. Then again, body horror is the apprehension of an internal threat; not the other way around.

#54
STUCK

2007

A woman commits a hit-and-run, then finds her fate tied to her victim.

6/8

With such a simple premise, I was surprised and impressed to notice that no film prior to 2007 comes close to Stuck narratively and stylistically. Nothing out there feels quite like it. It's an imaginative take on familiar tropes, but Stuart Gordon offers the kind of imagery that turns an otherwise quintessential psychological thriller into a gory horror film.

This is the story of a hit-and-run gone wrong, where the victim fights for his life and the driver wishes he'd just die. The accident is brutal and elaborate. There is black humor so black it's not even humor. But you'll laugh and feel bad for it if you're not dead inside. You'd think the victim is who you should root for, but he's not likable. The thing is, Mena Suvari isn't that likable either.

The exposition is thorough, so the fact that we don't care about either lead characters gives us the necessary distance to feel tension on both sides. Because we can't pick a side, we choose both. There's a handful of interesting subplots that don't connect the dots but make our characters deeper. All along, the writers ask the audience one question: what would you do?

WWW.TERROR.CA

#55
THE MUMMY RETURNS

2001

A re-animated mummy kidnaps a child who carries a powerful artifact.

6/8

You thought our heroes had it hard in 1999's The Mummy? Wait till you've met The Scorpion King! Brendan Fraser and Rachel Weisz's characters are now an old couple and have a child who joins them on their archaeological trips. He gets kidnapped, early on, and needs to be rescued by his parents who are now somehow chosen ones, something the original film forgot to tell us.

Like its predecessor, The Mummy Returns is very reminiscent of the Indiana Jones films. In true adventure film fashion, the film exploits all means of transportation left unscripted. We visit vast landscapes and travel the world with beautiful computer generated scenery. The first half of the movie is a condensed version of Part 1 and the second one a whole new bag of surprises.

All the dialogue and flashbacks related to past lives ranges from laughable to annoying. It reveals a flawed script. The computer generated effects are still terrible. The franchise doesn't lose too much momentum, though; it sticks to the formula while introducing new elements. This one plays a little more like a video game and less like a horror film. It is a little slow but has a great finale.

#56
THE BUTTERFLY EFFECT 2

2006

A man realizes he can travel back in time and alter the present by looking at pictures of himself.

6/8

The main protagonist, here, deserves a bit of his bad fortune. Contrary to Ashton Kutcher's character, in the first film, Eric Lively's character is superficial and uses his powers to achieve frivolous goals. His ambitions are mostly professional. He doesn't value life and can't appreciate his girlfriend. He isn't that likable and certainly not relatable, but his story is interesting nonetheless.

With this new installment, this emerging franchise ages surprisingly well. This sequel is both similar and different enough from the original that it is worth watching. It does't feel redundant and is supported by a decent script. It hits the same sad notes Part 1 did, though more moderately, and features convincing actors who match the collective talent the original cast had.

The Butterfly Effect 2 exploits themes such as friendship, love, money, the ego, adulthood, business, regrets, suffering and death. Perhaps the film doesn't use its gimmick as much as it should. It certainly doesn't use it as much as the original movie did. The hero uses his powers like they're a genie in a bottle instead of truly trying to fix the past to avoid collateral tragedies.

WWW.TERROR.CA

#57
MY NAME IS BRUCE

2007

A B movie actor is chosen by villagers to fight a Chinese god.

6/8

I get what this film tries to accomplish, and it succeeds maybe half the time. It's about "Bruce Campbell being the best actor of his generation". This is a bold statement, but if you somewhat agree, you're going to love this. You get tons of Evil Dead Easter eggs and cameos. And, of course, you get Bruce Campbell doing his shtick. He's the arrogant BC you might have met in horror conventions.

Two things play against this film: the low budget and that annoying southern band narrating the story. The special effects hit and miss, and the villain is weirder than it is scary. If you have no clue who Bruce Campbell is, this isn't for you, but if you do know him, you obviously love him, and you're going to have a blast! Pure moments of hilarity await. You're going to need a diaper.

I laughed my way through this movie then, and I still do. Campbell plays a fifty-year-old teenage trailer-trash drunk who's slowly losing his fandom. No one cares about his shitty movies, and especially not his 2.0 love interest who's never seen them. The exposition is fantastic; the third act? Well, let's not talk about the third act. Hail to the king, baby!

#58
CABIN FEVER

2002

Isolated in a cabin in the woods, a group of friends become infected by a fast spreading disease.

6/8

If Cabin Fever at first behaves like any horror movie taking place in a remote cottage, it in fact finds its identity in that the main threat is an infectious disease. It starts simply enough with friends, including couples, seemingly supportive of each other but, then, traitors to each other when in jeopardy. The actors do a fine job with a vacillating script and sometimes odd dialogue.

The humor, here, is somewhat derived of inside jokes that we don't always fully get. It's a style, but it's consequently amateurish in its presentation. Paranoia, isolation and contagion are the fears the film plays on, and it's excellent at it. Between what you see, what is suggested and what you imagine, gore reminds you that this isn't just a psychological thriller.

The disease spreads so fast that it is played for a cringe and a laugh. By its raging scope, the plague is depicted as some impersonal slasher icon, with proper pacing, structure and body count. The sets, the score and the photo are reminiscent of similar subgenres, but, under this lens, the material is fresh enough on its own to generate something unique, entertaining, funny and sinister.

#59
JASON X

2001

A cryogenized revenant is thawed in a spaceship lab, returns to life and starts murdering the crew.

6/8

Let's face it: this is the Aliens version of Friday the 13th. It might as well be titled "Jason in Space" and, on those terms, it fills its mandate. It is highly tongue in cheek, aware of what it is and what it was, but if you can accept that you're up there; aboard a space ship and in a far future, no less, you might enjoy the ride. This apple, in fact, falls closer to the tree than instigated.

It borrows every imaginable cliché and uses any good enough excuse to throw Jason in extreme, fantastic situations, something that's increasing in the franchise. So, we have an undead berserker hunting a robot nudist and a bunch of horny teens. It's reminiscent of Crystal Lake in the 80's and a true tour-de-force! Most of the classic candy is brought back in one form or another and silver coated.

You might end up wishing Jason X went in space but deeper than the Alien franchise did or at least elsewhere. The film has ambition, ideas, but just wants to have fun with a refreshed gimmick rather than reinventing the wheel. The gory moments are abundant. Here, Jason gets a special treatment. He arguably gets one of his best designs to date and the camera loves him for it.

#60
EIGHT LEGGED FREAKS

2002

A town is being overrun by giant mutated spiders.

6/8

Because no other reference comes to mind, I'll call this is a supersized version of Arachnophobia, where everything is bigger, funnier, and more intense. The 3D spiders look fake, but this being a slapstick comedy, we tend to be more forgiving. It's also an action film. It has an incessant pacing and an enthralling score that keeps you on your toes.

Once shit hits the fan, there's no way to stop this thing. It's an epic roller-coaster ride. The deaths are non-lethal, so the gore is minimal. We never get confirmation that anyone dies. This is the kind of film everybody wanted to make and see in the 1950s, but with today's technology. It's an abundance of special effects that weren't possible then.

We get an assortment of colorful actors playing vibrant characters. We're talking David Arquette, Kari Wuhrer, Doug E. Doug, and Scarlett Johansson. The producers trusted inexperienced screenwriter and director Ellory Elkayem with a reasonable budget and he pulled it off nicely. This is a B movie disguised as a blockbuster. It's not for everyone, but it's accessible, nonetheless.

#61
TEETH

2007

A pubescent teenager discovers her vagina has teeth.

6/8

Teeth is a cautionary tale that strongly encourages teens to keep their hands in their pockets and far away from the Devil. It's a coming of age story memorable for two things: its set pieces and an angry vagina we never get to see. Our imagination does all the work. In fact, writer and director Mitchell Lichtenstein is more interested in penises. Chopped-up penises.

Several establishing shots of a power plant strongly suggest that Dawn, played by Jess Weixler, has mutated from nearby radiations. Her vagina has a set of teeth and that's not cool. Weixler is plausible as the religious virgin with a purity ring. At least, that's who we're introduced to. She has a strong arc. Her story is tragic despite the tongue-in-cheek approach to her ludicrous disease.

This is a movie that will undoubtedly alienate the average male but will surely rub feminists the right way. That being said, it's probably the best way to tell this story. What's more, considering all the sex we see on the media, it's interesting to actually tackle the subject intellectually. This isn't sex ed 101. It's the stuff they forgot to teach you in high school.

#62
LESBIAN VAMPIRE KILLERS

2009

A pack of lesbian vampires attack a group of tourists, hoping to capture a virgin.

6/8

With a title like this one, you'd expect boobs at every turn and people screwing in every position. This is not that movie. Nudity is minimal. What you get, though, is beautiful women; nines and tens, in sexy outfits moving to the sound of Dance Mix 95. This starts out like every straight man's wet dream, and it pretty much plays this card long after shit hits the fan.

Even those not particularly fond of vampire films might enjoy Lesbian Vampire Killers the way From Dusk till Dawn pleased most audiences. It's a good slapstick comedy, first and foremost, it's extremely gory, but the monsters bleed white, so you could almost show this to a tween. But don't. This is a very sexual film with hints of Evil Dead and Dead Alive.

The actors are talented and funny. The special effects are convincing. The cinematography is highly dynamic. The only thing missing, here, is lesbians. Pretending that these vampires are lesbians doesn't make it so. I prepared for tons of lesbian sex and what I got, in return, is the story of a virgin. Nah, seriously... this film is pretty good. Just don't let the marketing fool you.

WWW.TERROR.CA

#63
BUBBA HO-TEP

2002

Two elders fight for their lives in a nursing home haunted by a mummy.

6/8

This is a small cast. The film is shot all in one place, backstories aside. Bruce Campbell plays Elvis Presley... or one of his impersonators. The script is never clear about it. Campbell gets the best lines. He's a caricature of himself "with a growth on his pecker". Ossie Davis plays his friend, who thinks he's JFK. A black JFK. As hilarious as this may be, it exposes the sad truth about aging.

Bubba Ho-Tep is a dark comedy, but it has an alarming subtext. The theme of aging in a culture that only values youth is downright depressing. After all, Bruce Campbell is the Elvis Presley of horror fans. Watching him stuck in bed or using a walker to move around is as funny as it is disconcerting. Despite its childish humor, Bubba Ho-Tep is brutally honest.

This is based on a novella by the same name. Sometimes, writer and director Don Coscarelli relies on visions in quick successions to convey the villain's backstory and it doesn't work. It's annoying and it breaks the flow. Elvis' flashbacks, on the other hand, are very amusing. This is a fun film with a cool score that's just right and adds to the ambiance.

#64
JEEPERS CREEPERS II

2003

High school students are attacked by a flying creature on a deserted road.

6/8

The Creeper strikes again and gets more screen time as the monster we now know him as. His mythology has been laid out and turned the original film into a complex subgenre cross-over but apparently left little for this sequel to chew on. Jeepers Creepers 2 goes full slasher. It doesn't go for subtlety and is rougher around the edges, from the screenplay to the photography.

Victor Salva can't seem to match the quality of Part 1. There are more characters but they share one personality. They aren't as relatable, not authentic and don't come with a backstory. They are as generic as this sequel is. It doesn't have the clever structure its predecessor had and the actors aren't invested as much, but, as a teen slasher, it meets most 80's genre standards.

Most of the story happens in and around a yellow bus in the middle of a deserted road with victimized high school boys because that's what the Creeper likes. The new premise is interesting and the delivery sometimes just as much, but this is a cold film with wobbly build-up, misplaced humor, stoic action scenes and awkward bits that ultimately deduct from our predisposition to fear.

#65
SWEENEY TODD: THE DEMON BARBER OF FLEET STREET

2007

A cook turns a barber's clients into meat pies.

6/8

I can't believe someone finally figured out how to turn this dusty tale into something great and worth viewing more than once. How exactly do you pay homage to an old musical play when adapting it into a feature film? Making it a musical was the way to go. This story was never meant to be taken seriously. It is artsy, it's a small story and the songs are basically compressed dialogue.

Tim Burton directs and that's good news. Johnny Depp and Helena Bonham Carter are a legendary pair. Alan Rickman and Timothy Spall, as the judge and the beadle, complete the dream team. Acting-wise, this is a masterpiece. The photography is peculiar; extremely textured and always lit to perfection. The only problem with this film originates from the source material: the songs aren't all earworms.

So, there you have it; a nearly perfect musical film hindered by a thin plot and arguably poor songs directed by one of the best artists of all time. The characters are unhinged. The humor is extremely dark. The gore is abundant but sparse. The screenplay fleshes out two overlapping tragic love stories, making this a memorable melodrama. This is a must see for fans of horror musicals.

#66
SALEM'S LOT

2004

The residents of a small town are gradually being converted to vampires.

6/8

Salem's Lot is the second adaptation of Stephen King's novel about a small town dealing with a vampire infestation. This 3 hour long delight keeps you guessing who gets converted to the undead next, until the remaining townsfolk decide to take action. King approaches the subject as maturely and realistically as possible. The filmmakers give us nothing less than an epic vampire tale.

It features a wide collection of characters played by excellent actors, with Rob Lowe as the main protagonist. He is a writer revisiting a troubled past who stumbles upon worse than he expected to find. Flashbacks make this movie sometimes more tedious to watch than it should be. It is otherwise one of the best TV adaptations of King's material. A significant budget went into it.

Exposition is what you get for most of the running time, which makes the second half a sad and tragic experience. The characters we used to care for turn one by one into creatures of the night and we, in return, feel growing desperation. The film is dialogue heavy but these words are not empty. Salem's Lot is a must-see for any fan of vampire movies and for all Stephen King completists.

#69
THE TEXAS CHAINSAW MASSACRE

2003

After a stranger committed suicide in their van, a group of friends looking for help become the targets of cannibals.

6/8

This is a remake of the 1974 horror cult classic about an insane Texas family of cannibals, though this could be said about the three last sequels to The Texas Chain Saw Massacre. Continuity has never worried the writers before, and this new release is no exception, though it brings back the darkness of the two first films. It plays it visceral and keeps it somewhat "Grindhouse".

Super-polished, well shot, and is highly color-corrected, it offers a whole new level of visual flair. The comedic elements of the previous two films are ignored and the story feels more real, this time around. Although some of the crazies we meet aren't as eccentric as we'd like them to be, others even things out a little. This time, we're going for scares and not so much for cheese.

The Texas Chainsaw Massacre hits a very dark note, early on, and turns into an increasing nightmare that is terrifying because it is so plausible, so relatable. It plays on the fear of strangers, of "others". Here's another deliberately depressing torture story of hillbillies and hitchhikers that, apart from a weak third act, gracefully homages one of the pillars of gritty slasher horror.

#70
THE TEXAS CHAINSAW MASSACRE: THE BEGINNING

2006

A mentally challenged orphan is raised by cannibals who prey on tourists.

6/8

This prequel to the 2003 The Texas Chain Saw Massacre remake by the same name, and to the franchise to some extent, revisits some concepts we're now taking for granted. We watch just how Leatherface came to be. As we learn, abortion, bad parenthood, poverty, mental illness and working in a slaughterhouse made him the sociopath we know. It's easy to buy. The script makes its point then moves on.

The backstory covers mostly Leatherface and his father, the impostor sheriff the film really revolves around. The character of Jessica Biel not returning, by default, more screen time is given to R. Lee Ermey. Every line he delivers is either insulting or terrifying, yet he can make audiences burst in nervous laughs, protected by the screen. He contributes to a highly immersing torture thriller.

It's one thing to build a large franchise around a resilient family of maniacs; another to tell its prequel while making sense of it all, considering all sequels were actually remakes, not continuity. The photography, the action scenes and the visceral gore are a cookie-cut of the last movie, but the film deliberately give us more of what we expected the first time around, almost as an apology...

WWW.TERROR.CA

#71
THE HITCHER

2007

A couple traveling on a deserted road comes across a dangerous hitchhiker.

6/8

You can watch this without having seen the original and your experience will not suffer from it. What we lost is surrealism, what we gain is composited aesthetic. The Hitcher remake is a solid thriller with excellent performers, good tension and impeccable photo. This is as Hollywood as horror gets. It's highly competent despite some bad editing room judgment calls.

The new John Ryder is as threatening as he needs to be through his actions, his body language, and his facial gesture. He is terribly confident, dominant. He could just as well be a business man. He's smart, charismatic, which adds to the mystery he gradually puts us through. His paradoxical motivations are never made very clear and his resourcefulness is depicted as borderline supernatural.

The biggest script difference between the 1986 version and this is that we now have a couple of protagonists caring for their lives and each other, both introduced early in the movie. The love axis was forced in, the first time around, and feels more natural now. It also creates ongoing dialogue, but then it also takes away from the unique macho mano-a-mano vibe some might have expected to return.

#72
SILENT HILL

2006

A woman searches for her daughter in a desolate town.

6/8

Silent Hill is the adaptation of a legendary video game series by the same title. Like the games, it is all style, all ambiance and low substance. It is both admirable and destabilizing. Unusual characters meet in unusual places. Ashes permanently fall from the sky and are almost ignored by the protagonists. The effects are at times amazing and at times so cheap they lose their fright factor.

It features monsters indescribable with words; midway between ghosts and revenants. The Archvillain, Pyramid Head, is a work of art. His design is wonderful yet terrifying. The weakest part of the film is that its two main investigations and its various flashbacks sometimes feel forced. This said, those subplots eventually converge and end up being worth the investment... because we need a story.

Like a map from a horror video game, the haunted town is delimited by locked fences, collapsed roads and other obstacles convenient for writers. This film is a great mindfuck with hints of sadness, loneliness and terror. It has a unique atmosphere that perfectly reflects the source material. All things considered, it is easily one of the best horror game adaptions of all times!

#73
FEAST

2005

Patrons locked inside a bar are attacked by monsters.

6/8

Everyone in this is too cool for school; all introduced with a text description that doesn't mean much but sets the tone. Their names and a combination of their occupations, reputations, "vibes", skills, life expectancy and fun facts are listed. It sure looks like the cast and crew had fun on the set. This is the result of the third season of project Greenlight, an amateur filmmaking reality show.

But this doesn't feel amateur at all! Some aspects of it are even ground-breaking, like an ill-defined antagonist and stereotypical characters with unintuitive arcs. The gore is excessive and imaginative. Rarely have we had so much fun with blood since Evil Dead 2 and Dead Alive. We're in a constant loop, oscillating between tension, jump scares, frantic action, splatter and physical comedy.

Everything that can possibly make sense or follow logic, here, eventually collapses and turns into a joke. Victims that are badly injured don't necessarily die; a rarity in movies considering this sort of visual continuity demands a lot from make-up artists and directors. The movie's not perfect; it is emotionally detached from us, is roughly edited, somewhat random, but it sure is memorable.

#76
ROSE RED

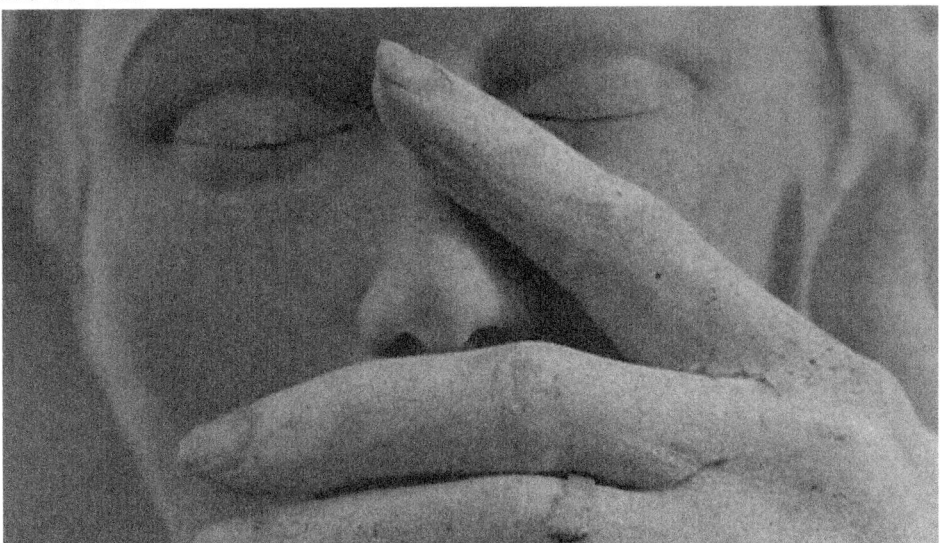

2002

A paranormal researcher gathers a group of psychics to rekindle spirits inhabiting a shape shifting house.

6/8

As explained in early scenes, Rose Red is a haunted house that grows on its own by feeding on human life. It is, in a way, a shape shifting labyrinth. Though it is a quintessential Stephen King trademark, having every protagonist be a psychic casts a shadow on the supernatural threat. In horror film history, this trope has been known to cause disinterest rather than scaring the audience.

Like any script faithful to Stephen King's original material, the dialogue is peculiar, a little off and doesn't flow naturally. The characters don't feel like they're from our plausible world, but the acting is not the issue. We get a good cast of familiar faces and intense deliveries. The flashbacks and retelling of the past blend in well and add layers of depth.

The first half is all exposition and apprehension. The real build-up starts at the mid-point, as the plot is transported inside the haunted mansion. This is a mini-series and, although you can tell by a photography too fluid and occasional low-key lighting, it features various impressive effects that create an unusually strong illusion for a production of this type.

#77
THE DESCENT: PART 2

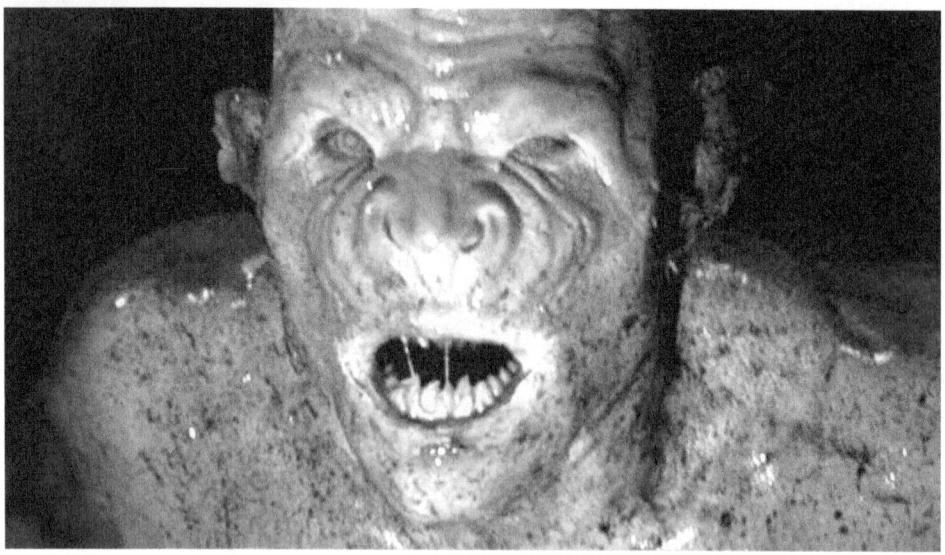

2009

An amnesic woman explores the cave she escaped from before being hospitalized.

6/8

The Descent 2 starts in a great deal of confusion, with its main protagonist Sarah in an amnesic state, hospitalized and bombarded by a police investigation shortly following the events of Part 1. The police convince Sarah to explore the caves, once again, which leaves us wondering what exactly there is left to discover there. We had pretty much everything covered the first time around...

Her amnesia is convenient. Nothing else would make her go back. Like the first movie, this one has gore and vicious jump scares. It is highly suspenseful and unpredictable. It is generally more of the same but contains a few pleasing surprises. The creature effects are still excellent and we see a bit more of them, this time around. We center more on them, now, than on mere claustrophobia.

It is rare and refreshing to watch a horror adventure with action and no romance. Part 2 may be replicating the original film, but by doing so it is giving the fan what they want. The stripped away the weird parts, all the fun, and maximized the horrifying aspects. On a technical level, the film is irreproachable. The actors are just as good but their characters just turned into caricatures.

#78
ABOMINABLE

2006

A man in a wheelchair spending time in the woods believes Bigfoot exists.

6/8

If you're an average horror fan, you probably have a checklist when it comes to finding the ultimate scary movie. Abominable is everything a classic should be. It contains a balanced amount of gore, jump scares, suspense and boobs. It never stagnates. When it's not a psychological thriller, it's a creature feature or an amazing slasher. It is, simply put, one of the best Bigfoot movies out there.

As if it couldn't get any cooler, Abominable is, in fact, a scream queen and king reunion. Jeffrey Combs is unrecognizable, Lance Henriksen is a smart ass, and Tiffany Shepis has a short but memorable presence. There are other familiar faces, but the budget is humble and so is the casting. These are the kind of actors we'd get in a 1980s horror b-movie, and that's all we need.

The filmmakers slowly reveal their monster. First, the footsteps, then a newspaper headline, followed by an abduction and, just before shit hits the fan, Henriksen finds a cave with animal remains. Things start slowly but escalate quickly. The Bigfoot is a man in a suit with CG eyes, but it's very convincing and it looks bad ass. Abominable is at times Hitchcockian and at times extremely cheesy.

#79
VALENTINE

2001

Five women are stalked by a masked individual before Valentine's Day.

6/8

Valentine is polished the way Scream was. In fact, without Scream, there is no Valentine. Katherine Heigl, David Boreanaz, Denise Richards and Marley Shelton play significant roles. All the young actors look conveniently good and everyone's flirting or in serious dating mode, yet they're surprisingly hostile to each other. The film is misandrist. Men are either alcoholic, poor, stupid, or creeps.

This is a whodunit slasher. The killer's identity isn't exactly protected by the script. There are several red herrings, but the suspects all get murdered early on, so only few options remain. The movie starts with an elaborate murder scene and ends with a lengthy house party scene, just like Scream. Indeed, Valentine is very formulaic, but the formula has been tested and it works.

This is a clean slasher. The gore is limited. The dialogue is elegant. The set design is gracious. The score is prominent. It's a fascinating, sugar-coated and nerve-racking film with good pacing and convincing effects. It has virtually no slow moments, but it's not hectic either. The script is character-oriented and dialogue-driven. It grows on you.

#80
VACANCY

2007

A couple becomes stranded at an isolated motel and finds hidden cameras in their room.

6/8

In Vacancy, Kate Beckinsale and Luke Wilson offer the kind of performances that make you forget you're watching fiction. The story makes us reflect on the times we took our lover for granted. It is a reverse home invasion flick in that the action takes place in a hotel whose rooms are rigged with cameras. The antagonists' motivations are a mystery to us for most of the running time.

The first third is an enigma that slowly unveils and soon turns into a traveler's worst nightmare. At times we relate to situations of jealousy and of regrets. At other times we feel as vulnerable as the protagonists, unable to think of an escape plan. Vacancy is an excellent mix of terror, action and sadness. The film is shot with a handful of actors and pretty much one location.

Well shot and well directed, with its many intrigues, Vacancy keeps us on the edge of our seat from beginning to end. The screenplay is more or less realistic, and we wonder how grade A actors accepted it in the first place. The last act has answers to our questions. Some are hard to swallow. Overall, you'll have a good time, here. Try not to overthink what you see.

WWW.TERROR.CA

#81
BLACK CHRISTMAS

2006

During their Christmas vacation, the residents of a sorority house are stalked by a psychopath who escaped from a mental asylum.

6/8

Although this is a remake of a 1974 film, a prolonged introduction would have us think it is in fact a sequel. This said, the story is pretty much the same. Better structured than its predecessor, it uses the best of current technology and offers densely detailed photography, precise editing and cunning lighting setups. This is an enhanced version of the stuff more generic slashers are based on.

Fans of the original might question the increased abundance of backstory pertaining to the killer. This is new territory but it doesn't necessarily feel out of place, although it kills the mystery. Fortunately, the film is well paced, suspenseful when it needs to be and never loses your attention. For a slasher, there is little sex or nudity and the story is surprisingly dense... too dense, perhaps.

If you overlook the plastic performances and the formatted script, you'll be pleased by Black Christmas. Simply put, it is the ultimate non-supernatural, though surreal, Christmas-themed horror movie. Don't expect an evil Santa Claus with powers, but rather a brute that wraps itself in a great omnipresent visual holiday ambiance before assaulting you with clever jump scares.

#82
P2

2007

A woman is pursued by a psychopath after being locked in a parking garage on Christmas Eve.

6/8

P2 is as simple as thrillers get, but it has some qualities that make it stand out. It has no supernatural element, but it takes place on Christmas Eve. It stars two actors, mainly, and they're excellent. Wes Bentley is very credible as the psychopath and we're 110% behind Rachel Nichols' character. The third big player is the parking garage itself. It has a vibrant palette of aqua and reds.

If we didn't take her situation seriously enough from the get go, Nichols' character does a good job of conveying just how much trouble she's in and how menacing her assailant appears to be. Her situation is so out of proportion that we, as an audience, are baffled and disoriented. Her fear guides us. Bentley's character can't be reasoned with and often resorts to gaslighting.

This is not a movie that defines or prides itself by its gore, but it's very graphic when it decides to be. It's a psychological horror thriller that really embraces both genres. It has the photography, acting level and special effects of a blockbuster, but it was probably made for much less than one, considering the size of the cast and the fact that it was pretty much shot in one location.

#83
CHERRY FALLS

2000

Someone is killing off the virgins of a high school.

6/8

In the spirit of Scream, I Know What You Did Last Summer, and Urban Legend comes an underdog that deserves your attention. The cast is composed of good-looking twenty-something playing teenagers with attitudes. The dialogue à la Kevin Williamson is almost always flirtatious and too elaborate to flow. The creators made it a mission to glamorize murder, which has been a trend since 1996.

Brittany Murphy plays the least stereotyped final girl imaginable. She's strange. Everyone is. All characters are eccentric in their own way. This serves three purposes: throwing red herrings, reaching a young audience, and replicating the success of the recent wave of slashers. This film has a weird vibe, and it's hard to blame it on one thing specifically.

Since the murderer kills off virgins, we get an awkward conversation between Brittany Murphy and her father where he pretty much rushes her to have sex. Murphy kisses her mom not once but twice on the mouth. We get entire scenes of extended suspense meant to exonerate potential killers and it's not subtle. This film, as good as it is, protects its twist poorly.

#84
RED DRAGON

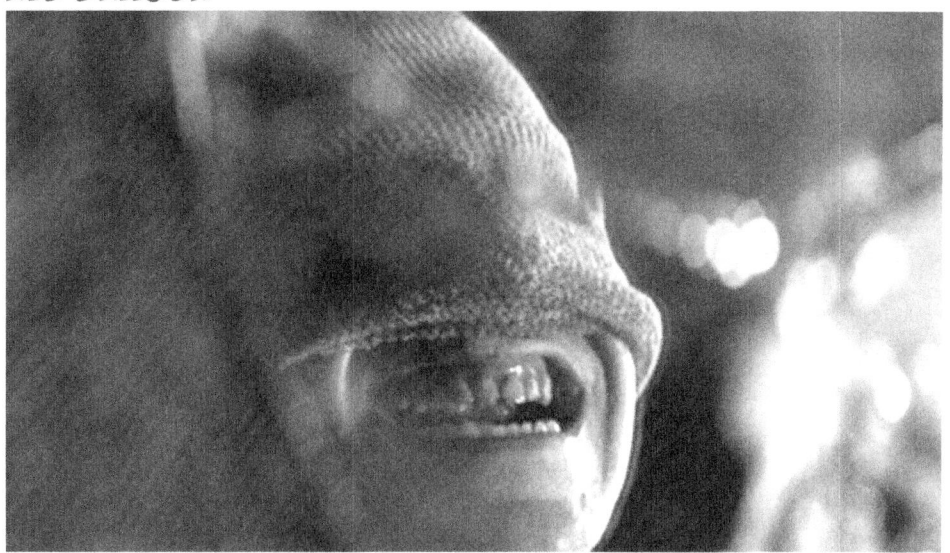

2002

Assisted by a dangerous cannibal, a former FBI agent helps catch an elusive serial killer.

6/8

Different high caliber directors took a stab at Thomas Harris' Hannibal Lecter novels. Red Dragon is the second adaptation of the first book by the same name. 1986's Manhunter was a decent first attempt but it didn't benefit from Anthony Hopkins' presence and felt cheap. Like Silence of the Lambs and Hannibal, Red Dragon brings back the grade A actor that made the series a success.

Silence of the Lambs is vaguely used as a template, here, putting drama at the forefront and gore far behind. The antagonist is infinitely more fleshed out than Buffalo Bill was. Ralph Fiennes doesn't exactly inspire fear and strength, but he can sure play crazy. Lecter is faithful to the man we've now come to enjoy as a horror icon and is still an unlikely reversal on superheroes tropes.

We spend a lot of time with the bad guys and not so much with the bleak Edward Norton, who never fully convinces us he can think like a murderer. This isn't the best entry so far, but it's a strong one that truly digs into the mind of a schizophrenic time-bomb. Despite an odd pacing and counter-intuitive storytelling, we get yet another dark, minimalist but satisfying thriller.

#85
DOLAN'S CADILLAC

2009

A man attempts to avenge his wife's death after she is murdered by a mobster.

6/8

There is a good reason why this film's title alludes to someone's vehicle, and it's up to you to find out. When you finally get it, you'll smirk. You'll smirk twice, in fact; at the end of the first act and all through the last act. This is a quintessential revenge thriller with a pinch of surrealism. Like many adaptations of Stephen King's work, it is both sad and terrifying; a deadly formula.

This is a frustrating film. Christian Slater is the main attraction, here. He's the man we love to hate. It was a daring decision to put a big star in the antagonist's shoes, but it works. Wes Bentley's character wants him dead after he killed his girlfriend. He knows he's weak. His enemy seems invincible. He'll take imaginative detours to achieve his goal... and this is where King's magic happens!

The plot is exaggerated. The main protagonist's master plan is far-fetched, but it is poetically ironic. While you may underestimate this flick, at first glance, from its marketing, its title and its premise, you will be cheering by the time the end credits roll. This is not King's most eccentric story, but it's a memorable one. It's modest, plausible and easy to relate to.

#86
THE LAST HOUSE ON THE LEFT

2009

Two teenagers are kidnapped, tortured and raped by a dysfunctional family of criminals.

6/8

The first four things that may strike you about this remake, if you're familiar with Wes Craven's version, is the quality of the cast and how differently the antagonists, although still criminals and rapists, are portrayed. Everybody looks good, not dirty. This is also a visibly high-end production; no longer a grindhouse. Lastly, the scenario is denser, more intricate and more layered.

The performances are of the highest standard and the dialogue just as solid. Now, you might wonder how a script can afford grade A actors, rape and nudity all in the same film, repeatedly. Well, it doesn't. It's not as visually shocking as you'd expect, but it conveys its suspense and horror brilliantly through what you what you think you see; not what you actually do. Wise use of audio helps.

It can both titillate and disgust you, sometimes all at once, then makes you feel bad about the voyeur it turns you in. The touchy subject might trigger bad memories or phobias. Some will simply appreciate that a big production ventured in sexual crimes and taboos, something rarely attempted. In the end, what you get is a rape revenge flick with an actual story, good taste and reasonable pacing.

#87
MAY

2002

A lonely traumatized woman attempts to make friends.

6/8

There's a cute creepiness about Angela Betis that makes this film work. It's hard to imagine anyone else filing her shoes. Anna Faris is the second-best thing about May. She's a wonderful actress and she's the only funny presence in an increasingly sinister story. She plays a kinky lesbian who loves pain. It's too bad this aspect is never really fleshed out. Then again, this isn't porn.

Every second of this strange movie is an experience. May, the protagonist, had a rough childhood due to her lazy eye. Once she gets that fixed, she thinks she'll be accepted by society, so she starts flirting and only exposes herself for what she is: a freak. This movie is touching, fascinating, and the tension is close to inexistent despite a lot of violence towards the end.

Expect the kind of dark humor that rubs horror movie fans the right way. That being said, May is not a comedy. Since the "bad girl" is the protagonist, this movie isn't exactly scary. It is very well put together. It is brilliantly written, directed professionally, yet there is an ounce of amateurism to it, perhaps noticeable because of the small cast and the modest set design.

#88
SECRET WINDOW

2004

A writer is threatened by a man he supposedly plagiarized.

6/8

Johnny Depp plays in it, yet it is far from being one of Stephen King's best screen adaptations. It's about an alcoholic writer with a hot temper who is extremely lazy and who actually doesn't write all that much. A few surprises along the way make this film better than it first appears to be. It's a straightfoward story and it is a tad predictable. Depp is the best thing about it.

The cast, the shooting locations and the special effects are in limited amounts. Writer/director David Koepp keeps it simple. He shoots this film the way Hitchcock did; by having fun with the camera, by putting all his efforts on dialogue and by maintaining suspense. Writing, Jack Daniels, a motel, a killer; those elements are near and dear to Stephen King.

If you're a King completist, a young horror aficionado looking for a gateway, or if you like thrillers with a drop of horror, then this is a movie for you. The film is flawed but possesses many redeeming qualities, like the way it is structured so the audience can solve the mystery with clues intentionally scattered from beginning to end... and what an ending!

WWW.TERROR.CA

#89
SESSION 9

2001

A cleaning crew uncovers the dark past of an abandoned mental hospital they are working in.

6/8

I can almost guarantee you that one year after seeing this movie, you won't even remember how it ends. You'll be compelled, at some point, to watch it again and you might as well have been lobotomized. This film is extremely vague and darkly poetic. In a nutshell, Session 9 tells the story of a cleaning crew working in an abandoned mental hospital.

Session 9 is one of the best horror films in which nothing actually happens, at least nothing concrete that moves the plot forward. We're never sure we can trust what is being said and shown. The movie is a big blur. The piano score is bone-chilling. The actors are very talented. They give us the exact dynamic and attitude we expect from handymen: they're proud and rough around the edges.

The ambiance of this film by far exceeds its story structure. All we really need is a creepy looking place that would swallow the cast whole if it happened to be haunted... and it probably is. This story explores the fears of the dark, of being alone, the fear of illness and, ultimately, of ghosts. You can punch a vampire or a mummy in the face, but there isn't much you can do against a ghost.

#90
THE HOUSE OF THE DEVIL

2009

A young woman takes a strange babysitting job and soon regrets it.

6/8

Shot like it's right out of the 1970s, featuring a protagonist with a 1970s hairdo, a 1970s face and wearing 1970s clothes, The House of the Devil opens the way 1970s movies did. It is a slow-paced wonder. It is so slow it is basically filmed in real-time. We're in good company. The main actress, who we spend the most of our time with, is the girl next door.

The film reminds us of Rosemary's Baby. Not much happens in the second act, but that's fine. Jocelin Donahue carries this production on her shoulders. The other characters are necessary but this is not about them. Ultimately, Ti West is the reason The House of the Devil is fun to watch despite how minimalist it is, when all is said and done. He likes it this way. It's his signature.

Although it is very much inspired by films made 30 to 40 years prior, this flick is quite refreshing. It doesn't need a big budget and big names to appeal to audiences of all ages. It's the classic story of the babysitter and the stalker. You know this story. Let Ti West tell you once more, with his own twist. Let the intrigue sink in. This is one hell of a thriller.

#91
KING KONG

2005

A filmmaker looking for cheap production value coerces a ship crew into visiting an uncharted island.

6/8

Peter Jackson offers us his intricate and extended vision of 1933's King Kong. This is a slow and long adaptation that isn't boring, by any means, if you can appreciate the ensemble cast. It is a period piece with great sets, costumes, and astonishing photography. Each character is given plenty of exposition and treated somewhat like a caricature. Their performances are virtually flawless.

As a result, we care for them and their fate. Things get unexpectedly dark and violent in the second act. It hits us hard because it purposely isn't foreshadowed. The last King Kong pictures made use of practical effect only, but here the beasts are mostly CG. Their animation is convincing and the 3-D meshes are convincingly rigged, textured and lit. This isn't much of a horror movie, so it works.

The three acts are dense in detail; visually and narratively. There are strong key moments in the script that define and redefine the main characters through their actions and arcs. Their vices and skills will either play for or against them, or make them both protagonists and antagonists, at the same time or alternatively. This is an adaptation of epic proportions that complexifies simplicity.

#92
SAW V

2008

The survivor of a decimated cult forces a dangerous puzzle upon a handful of people, including a special agent that is tailing him.

6/8

The fifth installment in the Saw franchise spends time with serial killer Jigsaw's widow as she receives her mysterious inheritance. On the other hand, we get to know our newly established antagonist who carries the game master's legacy and we're not exactly sure why. The script simply doesn't offer plausible incentives. Somewhere in the middle of this, a group of people must cooperate to survive.

What used to be an ideology slowly turns into the elaborate criminal schemes of a corrupted cop. While we are far from the simplified complexity of 2004's Saw, we're given a refreshing game of dogs, cats and mice that the writers manage to keep interesting from beginning to end. This feels like a transitional sequel that ends where the last one stopped and sets the table for another installment.

Consequently, Saw V is hard to synopsize and appreciate on its own. It does live up to expectations, though, in regards to acting, writing and directing. You'll get what you expect, gore and creative torture devices included, but you might want to be up-to-date with the franchise before giving it a try. It is indissociable from its predecessors but pulls enough fresh intrigues to please the fan.

WWW.TERROR.CA

#93
TIMECRIMES

2007

A man accidentally gets into a time machine and travels back in time.

6/8

Timecrimes is brilliantly written but a bit predictable. It could be argued that it is too damn convoluted, but fans of time travel films enjoy complexity. It comes with the genre. The acting is a little off and the unintuitive dialogue doesn't help, but you get used to it. There's a healthy dose of humor. It is barely perceptible but it's there. Timecrimes is otherwise pretty dark.

This is about a man who gets stuck inside a time loop. We go through a variety of emotions. Just when you think this film is too sinister, things get technical and we get some science-fiction. Then, you get a sweet montage. This happens at the turn of the second act and the pacing picks up. Then, right around the middle of the story, as if things couldn't get weirder, the mind-fuck thickens.

The questions stack. Every answer brings up a new question. This goes on for a while. There is fatigue at various moments, but it never lasts. All in all, this film is a must-see. It's in its own category. It's extremely imaginative. It may very well be a gaping plot hole, but that's hard to tell. Time travel movies are always complicated and this one is no exception.

#94
28 DAYS LATER...

2002

Survivors of an infectious plague travel to find sanctuary.

6/8

The writers make it clear: this apocalyptic world is infested by humans infected by rage and not zombies. The difference? They run at you screaming, looking angry. They pose a great challenge to our characters; ruthless survivors well-aware of the dangers ahead and, our lead, a confused man who happened to be in a coma when the infestation stroke. We discover the devastated world as he does.

There is neither traffic nor sign of life in the streets of London. Many establishing shots show the city in apocalyptic mode; without a doubt a difficult task to accomplish for director Danny Boyle, especially around famous landmarks such as the Westminster Bridge. This may not be a zombie movie, per say, but it hits the same notes and presents a familiar screenplay.

Jerky high speed cameras are used for action scenes that the movie could've done without. Expect effective jump scares, strategic build-up and good suspense for the most part, though. This is a quintessential post-apocalyptic horror adventure feature in which true evil is revealed to be ugly human nature. This is the story of what happens when no one can protect you from rape, theft and murder.

WWW.TERROR.CA

#95
RESIDENT EVIL: APOCALYPSE

2004

A group of people attempt to evacuate a city plagued by zombies.

6/8

After some background story describing what destroyed Raccoon City, we pick up right after the events of Part 1 with Milla Jovovich's character attempting to survive a new hell. We now have two lead characters; two strong women, whose storyline eventually converge. The movie doesn't hold back on zombies and throws us right back in the mayhem before we can take our breath.

Action scenes are now more prominent, cooler and more elaborate but at the expense of build-up, atmosphere and suspenseful horror. The zombies are in greater number and there are virtually no slow moments. The subtle change in directing results in numerous jerky shots of monsters we'd rather watch unedited, and the occasional slow motion stunt right out of The Matrix. Sometimes, less is more...

The newly introduced villain, Nemesis, is a force to be reckoned with and redefines the word "fear". The photography is still of the highest standards, the acting irreproachable and the set design completely immersing. Though it sometimes indulges in post-production effects and vapid subplots, all things considered, Resident Evil: Apocalypse is a worthy sequel that meets most expectations.

#96
AVP: ALIEN VS. PREDATOR

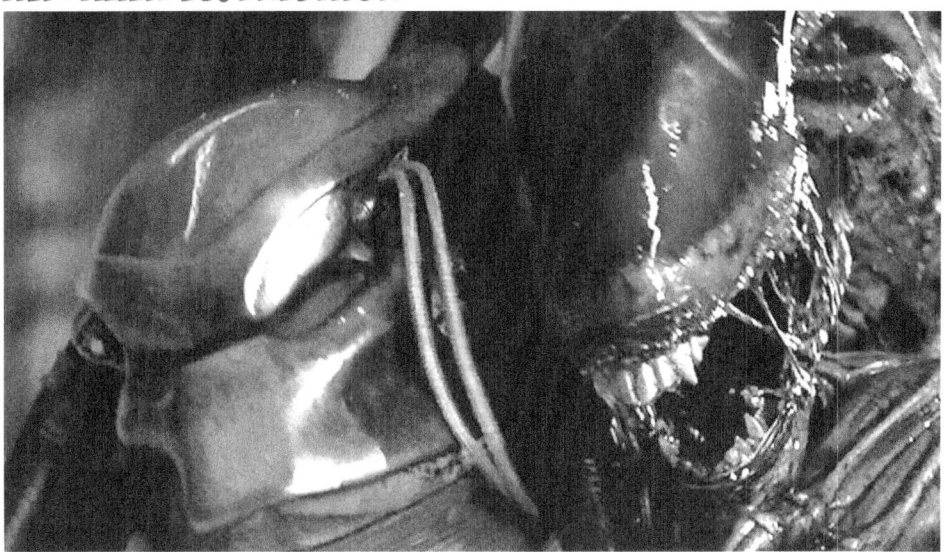

2004

A team of archaeologists explore a subterranean labyrinth and get caught up in a war between two alien races.

6/8

The best elements of AVP are its strong cast and its gorgeous set design. H.R. Giger provided outstanding artwork for the Alien franchise, and the ones featured in Predator 2, for instance, were not far from the hybrid we get here. The war between Alien and Predator takes place inside an underground pyramid that behaves like a self-solving 3D-Puzzle.

Freddy vs. Jason came out a year prior and was more into the "versus" aspect than character exposition. Both match-up spin-offs were born from rumors and fan fiction in the 80's, and took this long to come out. AVP can be a letdown for viewers with high expectations. It is the script that brings the movie down, sadly. Character arcs are limited by their uselessness as humans in the plot.

The creatures look great, and so does the production as a whole. The two franchises are treated with respect. The writers grasped the occasion to spend time discovering their villain and it pays off. The third act is weak and glorifies a human that simply doesn't deserve our gratification. The two villains aren't exactly vocal, so the conclusion is somewhat abrupt but reminiscent of slashers.

WWW.TERROR.CA

#97
JURASSIC PARK III

2001

A businessman's contribution to science grants him and his wife a tour on an island inhabited by dinosaurs.

6/8

Returning to the now desolated island after the urban backdrop of Part 2 was probably not the best way to go for this second sequel to a still unmatched classic that revolutionized CG and elevated production standards for blockbusters. Jurassic Park was never just about dinosaurs. It required the perfect alignment of arcs, surprises and subplot to be the masterpiece Part 3 isn't.

The cast is of average presence and mostly orbits around Sam Neill returning from Part 1 after an absence that hinders continuity. This time, Jeff Goldblum's is missing and the impact is the same. Sadly, much like the island, this franchise got neglected and now feels empty. They give us the spinosaurus, a species larger and more threatening than a T-Rex, but they take a lot away in return.

The characters sometimes get too philosophical, the kids can be annoying, and most personas are paper thin; revealing a writing style and direction not as strategic and natural as 1993's Jurassic Park's. When Jurassic Park 3 does things right, it is an exciting action-packed adventure with plenty of suspense, strong build-up and impressive eye-candy. As a sequel, though, it is under-cooked.

#98
THE BOX

2009

A couple are offered a million dollars if they press a button on a wooden box, understanding that will kill someone they do not know.

6/8

You press a button, you get a million dollars in cash and someone you don't know dies. That's a powerful premise. This short story by Richard Matheson was previously adapted into an episode of the 1980s iteration of The Twilight Zone. As a feature film, it runs dry in the second half. As you can expect, it turns into a procedural, passed a certain point, and becomes every other horror movie.

Some elements outside of the original scope eventually graft themselves. The initial gimmick is dissected. The situation is flipped up side down. We learn more than we need to know. Ignorance is bliss. Thankfully, things pick up during the last act. Frank Legella's character gains unsuspected dimensions, Cameron Diaz's character breaks our hearts and James Marsden... is James Marsden.

The Box is a period piece. It takes places in 1976. This adds an additional barrier between the us and the characters. In fact, this is a cold, distant film. Most characters are hostile. The arcs of the main characters are extremely tragic and hopeless. Dread and sadness go hand in hand in horror. Take away thirty minutes of this movie and you end up with a polished gem.

WWW.TERROR.CA

#99
SAW VI

2009

A member of a sadistic cult frames a FBI agent he killed for his own murders.

6/8

It's clear now: Jigsaw's plan was to kill everybody who propagated sadness, injustice and death around him. Much like the third and fourth films of the franchise, this one features a roughly developed and hardly relatable main protagonist who must save people he knows well; in this case a handful of colleagues as professionally vile as he is. He's a greedy insurance company suit; the kind we hate.

Familiar faces and buried secrets come back to the surface. Jigsaw's copycat follower is getting sloppier. While the few previous films felt continuous and focused on the bad guys' background, this one brings us back to a simpler plot. With most of the Jigsaw cult dead, it feels like the end is near, yet we're given a whole new cast of victims that end up postponing what should be concluded.

This is arguably the first time we're chasing our tail. While the script is nicely packaged, it could be said that Saw VI is all filler. It brings little to the global story and doesn't feel like a transition to a potential 6th sequel. The actors are a skilled bunch but their arc is inexistent. It's still a well shot horror film with a big budget, but it's one of the weakest entries so far.

#100
THE RING

2002

A journalist investigates a cursed videotape that causes death.

6/8

The Ring re-imagines Japanese horror success Ringu. It replicates the eerie urban ambiance of the original movie, setting its key scenes in small clustered American apartments. The deal-breaker for any Ringu completist is that the protagonists don't have supernatural powers. It takes us away from the more fantastic adaptations of the classic Japanese folk tale and novel, for better or worse.

It's better than your average haunting movie. For one thing, the ghost is confined to an infamous viral videotape that piques the curiosity of its victims and sets in motion a chain of events. It namely calls you to announce you'll die, when it will happen, then lets the protagonist struggle with apprehension and terror for a week. To us, the audience, this translates into an hour-long procedural.

The investigation Naomi Watt's character undertakes acts as preliminary to satisfying but sparse frights. There is little to no humor in The Ring. Build-up, ambiance and mystery are therefore at the forefront. To support it all is a genuinely creative tale that mixes ghost, supernatural contagion and technology, resulting in a powerful gimmick that justify an American remake.

WWW.TERROR.CA

FOR MORE HORROR-THEMED BOOKS, VISIT

WWW.TERROR.CA